Magdalena Baran-Szołtys, Monika Glosowitz,
Aleksandra Konarzewska (eds.)

Imagined Geographies

Central European Spatial Narratives between 1984 and 2014

Literatur und Kultur im mittleren und östlichen Europa

herausgegeben von Reinhard Ibler

ISSN 2195-1497

12   Julia Friedmann
     Von der Gorbimanie zur Putinphobie?
     Ursachen und Folgen medialer Politisierung
     ISBN 978-3-8382-0936-4

13   Reinhard Ibler (Hg.)
     Der Holocaust in den mitteleuropäischen Literaturen und Kulturen:
     Probleme der Politisierung und Ästhetisierung
     The Holocaust in the Central European Literatures and Cultures:
     Problems of Poetization and Aestheticization
     ISBN 978-3-8382-0952-4

14   Alexander Lell
     Studien zum erzählerischen Schaffen Vsevolod M. Garšins
     Zur Betrachtung des Unrechts in seinen Werken aus der Willensperspektive
     Arthur Schopenhauers
     ISBN 978-3-8382-1042-1

15   Dmitry Shlapentokh
     The Mongol Conquests in the Novels of Vasily Yan
     An Intellectual Biography
     ISBN 978-3-8382-1017-9

16   Katharina Bauer
     Liebe – Glaube – Russland:
     Russlandkonzeptionen im Schaffen Aleksej N. Tolstojs
     ISBN 978-3-8382-1182-4

17   Magdalena Baran-Szołtys, Monika Glosowitz,
     Aleksandra Konarzewska (eds.)
     Imagined Geographies
     Central European Spatial Narratives between 1984 and 2014
     ISBN 978-3-8382-1225-8

Magdalena Baran-Szołtys, Monika Glosowitz,
Aleksandra Konarzewska (eds.)

IMAGINED GEOGRAPHIES

Central European Spatial Narratives between 1984 and 2014

ibidem-Verlag
Stuttgart

Bibliografische Information der Deutschen Nationalbibliothek
Die Deutsche Nationalbibliothek verzeichnet diese Publikation in der
Deutschen Nationalbibliografie; detaillierte bibliografische Daten sind im
Internet über http://dnb.d-nb.de abrufbar.

Bibliographic information published by the Deutsche Nationalbibliothek
Die Deutsche Nationalbibliothek lists this publication in the Deutsche Nationalbibliografie;
detailed bibliographic data are available in the Internet at http://dnb.d-nb.de.

∞

Gedruckt auf alterungsbeständigem, säurefreien Papier
Printed on acid-free paper

ISSN 2195-1497
ISBN: 978-3-8382-1225-8

© *ibidem*-Verlag
Stuttgart 2018

Alle Rechte vorbehalten

Das Werk einschließlich aller seiner Teile ist urheberrechtlich geschützt. Jede Verwertung
außerhalb der engen Grenzen des Urheberrechtsgesetzes ist ohne Zustimmung des Verlages
unzulässig und strafbar. Dies gilt insbesondere für Vervielfältigungen,
Übersetzungen, Mikroverfilmungen und elektronische Speicherformen sowie die
Einspeicherung und Verarbeitung in elektronischen Systemen.

All rights reserved. No part of this publication may be reproduced, stored in or introduced into a retrieval
system, or transmitted, in any form, or by any means (electronical, mechanical, photocopying, recording or
otherwise) without the prior written permission of the publisher. Any person who does any unauthorized act
in relation to this publication may be liable to criminal prosecution and civil claims for damages.

Printed in the EU

Content

Acknowledgements 7

Aleksandra Konarzewska
Introduction. Central Europe and Its 30 Good Years (1984–2014) .. 9

Iris Llop
A Narrative Construction: The Idea of Central Europe in Milan Kundera's Writings 27

Jagoda Wierzejska
Galicia: An Eastern or a Western Land? Remarks on Locating the Province in the Framework of the East–West Opposition 51

Magdalena Baran-Szołtys
Andrzej Stasiuk's Galician 'Middle Europe': Half-Dark, Empty, and Boundless 87

Mariella C. Gronenthal
Longing for the Empty Space—Nostalgia and Central Europe 131

Author Information 147
Illustrations 151
Index of Names 155
Index of Subjects 161

ACKNOWLEDGEMENTS

The idea of the following volume originated at University of Tübingen in Germany during the workshop *Imagined Central European Geographies. Towards the Contemporary Politics of Location* (April 29–May 1 2016). The workshop was funded by the Institutional Strategy (*Exzellenzinitiative*) of the Graduate Academy of Tübingen (PSP Element: 404 100 1933), *Vereinigung der Freunde der Universität Tübingen*, and *Hölderlin Gesellschaft e.V.* We would hereby like thank all participants and supporters of this project, especially senior scholars from the Institute of the Slavic Languages and Literatures (University of Tübingen) and the Institute of Danube-Swabian History and Regional Studies—Tilman Berger, Gesine Drews-Sylla, Olivia Spiridon, and Schamma Schahadat—and our amazing keynote lecturers, Dirk Uffelmann (University of Passau) and Tamara Hundorova (National Academy of Sciences of Ukraine). Thank you again for your inspiring speeches, discussions, and feedback.

The concept of the volume changed in time, as we could consult our ideas with knowledgeable scholars and professionals. We are happy to express our gratitude to Jakob Horstmann who always believed in our project and patiently guided us through all steps of the publication process. We want to sincerely thank Marijeta Bozović, Krystyna Iłłakowicz, Kate Trumpener, Marci Shore, and Timothy Snyder (Yale University), Patrice Dabrowski (Harvard Ukrainian Research Institute), Zbigniew Kadłubek (University of Silesia), Annegret Pelz and Alois Woldan (University of Vienna). To Florian Bölter, Finn O'Branagáin, James Dunn, Karolina Kolpak, Zakhar Ishov, Suzanne May, Bronwyn Angela Miller, Amelia Smit, and Krystian Wojcieszuk we owe a debt of gratitude for their help with the final shape of the texts involved. Special thanks go to Michał Wasiucionek for his mordant yet always thought-provoking remarks on what Central Europe actually is.

M. B-S., M. G., A. K.

Aleksandra Konarzewska
University of Tübingen, Germany

INTRODUCTION. CENTRAL EUROPE AND ITS 30 GOOD YEARS (1984–2014)

Five years before the fall of the Berlin Wall, the Czech writer Milan Kundera published the essay *The Tragedy of Central Europe* in *The New York Review of Books*.[1] This short paper revived the concept of a European region 'between East and West' (which had been somewhat neglected during the Cold War), and established the critical framework for disputes concerning the region over the following decades. The term 'Central Europe' (or 'Middle Europe') refers to regions in eastern middle Europe that attempted to 'move to the West,' after the collapse of communism between 1989 and 1991, not only in terms of politics, but also in the spheres of economics and culture. Those attempts indeed succeeded in the majority of cases, but their rapid development was not linear, homogenous, or free of backlash.

The literature of this time, particularly spatial narratives, provides profound insights into the transformation processes of states from communism to capitalism in the regions of Central Europe. The slow disappearances of the mutual borders, the (re)invention of local / ethnic identities, and the complex multicultural past of regions such as Silesia or Galicia became popular literary motifs among Austrian, Ukrainian, and Polish authors. Nonetheless, the epoch of the continual westernisation processes in the region seems to be part of the past; the Russian military armed intervention in Ukraine in 2014 revived the East-West division of Europe and thus symbolically closed this era.

---

[1] Milan Kundera, "The Tragedy of Central Europe," *The New York Review of Books*, 31 (1984): 33–37. https://is.muni.cz/el/1423/jaro2016/MEB404/um/Kundera_1984.pdf (acc. October 6, 2017).

*

Figure 1: *The Austro-Hungarian Chaos* by Pierre de Coubertin (1902). Public Domain.

It should be noted that the terms 'Central Europe' and 'Middle Europe' carry specific connotations. The latter term particularly raises various issues; despite being a relatively neutral phrase in Slavic languages, it can also immediately evoke associations with the worst European experiences of the 20th century, as the concept of *Mitteleuropa* originated in German imperialism.[2] On the other hand, the idea of 'Central Europe' especially in its form of the 1980s and early 1990s, was a concept (or myth) of the intelligentsia. It was mostly popular among writers and dissidents in Poland, Czechoslovakia, and Hungary, and among Western intellectuals who were emotionally engaged with the region's situation.[3] Thus, the term also connotes: an idealisation of the past and quasi-utopian visions for the future,

---

[2] The canonical work *Mitteleuropa* by German theologian and politician Friedrich Neumann (1860–1919) was published during the First World War and presents the idea of Middle Europe as a project for the future: Friedrich Neumann, *Mitteleuropa* (Berlin: Verlag von Georg Reimer, 1916), https://archive.org/stream/mitteleuropa00naumuoft (accessed March 11, 2017).

[3] Cf. the enthusiastic opinions of the British historians Tony Judt and Timothy G. Ash: Tony Judt, Timothy Snyder, *Thinking the Twentieth Century* (New York, NY: Penguin Press, 2013); Timothy Garton, "Does Central Europe Exist?", in *In Search of Central Europe*. ed. George Schöpflin and Nancy Wood (Cambridge: Polity Press, 1989), 191–

intellectual impostures, the use of Big Words (such as 'Liberty' or 'Democracy'), and predispositions to moralisation.[4] Furthermore, 'Central Europe' implies the existence both of 'Western' and 'Eastern Europe,' where 'the West' (or 'Europe') refers to several different countries and stands for technical progress, wealth, civilization, and democracy, 'the East'—in accordance with classical Orientalism—is associated with backwardness, poverty, obscurantism, and a lack of personal freedom.[5]

---

215. For instance: 'I think that no reasonably sensitive Western observer encountering Central Europeans in the twentieth century could avoid that experience of unrequited love' in: Judt and Snyder, *Thinking the Twentieth Century*, 239; 'And yet I do believe that they [East Central European intelligentsia] have a treasure to offer us all. At their best, they give a personal example such as you rarely find in London, Washington, or Paris: an example, not of brilliance or wit or originality, but of intellectual responsibility, integrity, and courage' in: Timothy Garton Ash, 'Does Central Europe Exist?', 214. See also: Catherine Horel, "The Rediscovery of Central Europe in the 1980s" in *Fall of the Iron Curtain and the Culture of Europe*, ed. Peter I. Barta (New York, NY: Routledge, 2015) 24–39.

[4] Tony Judt, "The Dilemmas of Dissidence: The Politics of Opposition in East-Central Europe," *East European Politics & Societies* 2 (1988), 185–240; Zygmunt Bauman, "Intellectuals in East-Central Europe: Continuity and Change" in *In Search of Central Europe*. ed. George Schöpflin and Nancy Wood (Cambridge: Polity Press, 1989) 70–90. Cf. the much more deconstructive postcolonial approach in: Todorova, *Imagining the Balkans*, 293–334, as well as the gender-deconstructive portrait of *The Gloomy Writer* (i.e. a dissident writer from the *Ostblock*), and in the novel *Fording the Stream of Consciousness*. Dubravka Ugrešić, "GW, the Gloomy Writer," in *Thank you For Not Reading: Essays on Literary Trivia* (Normal, IL: Dalkey Archive Press, 2003) 105–9; Dubravka Ugrešić, *Fording the Stream of Consciousness* (London: Virago, 1991).

[5] In this respect *Eastern Europe* is a pejorative label similar to *the Balkans*: it denotes a region with which none would like to be identified: Todorova, *Imagining the Balkans*. Cf. a caustic comment from Joseph Brodsky on Milan Kundera: 'Having lived for so long in Eastern Europe (Western Asia to some), it is only natural that Mr. Kundera should want to be more European than the Europeans themselves.' In: Joseph Brodsky, "Why Milan Kundera Is Wrong About Dostoyevsky," *The New York Times*, February 17 (1985). http://www.nytimes.com/books/00/09/17/specials/brodsky-kundera.html (acc. March 11, 2017).

Figure 2: Postcard from Myslowitz/Sosnowitz (today: Mysłowice/Sosnowiec in Poland): Three Emperors' Corner. Depicted are: Nicholas II, Wilhelm II, Franz Joseph I (beginning of the 20th century). Public Domain.

It cannot be overlooked that 'Eastern Europe' defined in such a way that it only has one referent, i.e. Russia (or the Russian Empire, Soviet Union, or Russian Federation). This is the reason why various pleas for the use of 'Central Europe' are expressed mostly by the small countries of the former *Ostblock*, whose culture (as in the case of Czechia) or both culture and language (as in the case of Hungary) are different to Russian culture and language. A call to implement the term 'Central Europe' is effectively an act of protest against being identified with the local hegemon. On the other hand, those voices can often be reduced to emphasising the differences between Russia and non-Russian countries, often by way of stereotypes and resentments.[6] In short, introducing the term 'Central Europe' might be seen as a subtle way to apply the orientalising label 'Eastern Europe' to Russia only.[7]

---

[6] Cf. mixed reactions evoked by Kundera's article, especially the discussion between Egon Schwarz, Milan Šimečka, Jane Mellor, Mihàly Vajda, and Predrag Matvejević: Schöpflin and Wood, *In Search of Central Europe*, 143–90.

[7] In the words of Iver B. Neumann: 'The discourse on Central Europe was and is a moral appeal to Western Europe on behalf of an imagined community born of frustration with the Soviet hegemony in Eastern Europe.' In: Iver B Neumann, *Uses of the Other: "The*

So, why use this notion? The main reason can be simply summarised as terminological clarity. 'Central Europe' indeed implies the existence of Eastern Europe, which is almost automatically identified with Russia or the Soviet Union, and thus attempts to establish a difference between two cultural areas. This should not, however, be conceived in terms of cultural and linguistic hegemony among the states within Central Europe, but rather as a way of avoiding conceptual misunderstandings. The best example would be the cultural heritages of the two global powers of the 19th century, Austria-Hungary and the Russian Empire, which differed from each other in crucial spheres such as language, dominant religion, and social and economic structure. The significance of these differences should not be underestimated, especially considering that, for example, the era of *Kaisar* Franz Joseph I Habsburg lasted almost 70 years (1948–1916), or that the formal union of Austria and Hungary existed seven years longer than the postwar Cold War division of Europe. In other words, the differentiations implied by 'Central Europe' make it easier to grasp notions such as *fin de siècle* Prague or Budapest as having much more in common with Vienna and Paris than with St. Petersburg or Kiev.

East" in European Identity Formation (Minneapolis: University of Minnesota Press, 1999) 158.

Figure 3: The 'dream map' of Europe after the victory of Central Powers (by Alban Rumann, beginning of the 20th century). Public Domain.

Furthermore, the notion of 'Central Europe,' however imperfect, is highly useful when one wants to emphasize two particular qualities of this area: conceptual transformability and the potential of cultural inclusion. Conceptual transformability can be illustrated in the case of Switzerland: from the linguistic point of view, Swiss cantons can be seen as borderlands both of the Germanic and Romanic world. However, when applying a different criterion (for instance, the pre-modern one) it can be debated whether Switzerland belongs to the civilization of the European North (the culture of rye, beer, and butter) or South (the culture of wheat, wine, and olive oil). A similar transformability can be observed while discussing 'Central Europe.' For example, if one treats participation in the Latin and Greek Christian culture (or adopting the heritage of the Western and Eastern Roman Empires) as the crucial fault line between the Western and Eastern world, then not only Austria and Germany, but also such territories as Lithuania, Finland, and even vast parts of Ukraine will have to be considered as part of the Latin (i.e. Western) sphere of influence. This extension of the 'West' is also seen in: the oldest living traditions of Poland, Czechia, and Hungary are Latin;[8] having once been baptised in the Roman rite, people from Prague, Cracow, and Vilnius joined the world of people from Paris and Oxford; and at the same time participated in the crucial moments of the West's historical trajectory, such as the Reformation and the Thirty Years' War.[9] However, as soon as we shift our focus from religious criteria to linguistic ones, the boundaries change; the western part of the continent is then dominated by Romanic, Celtic and Germanic languages, while Slavic, Finno-Ugric and Baltic languages being prevalent in the East (the exceptional case being Romanian). Seen from this vantage point, the border between two parts of the continent can be drawn on the shores of the rivers Oder (the presentist approach) or Elbe (the genealogic approach).

The second quality of 'Central Europe,' the potential of cultural inclusion, is also not unique; it is present in other borderland parts of Europe, for instance in Sicily. This Mediterranean island has been influenced by the Greek, Roman, Byzantine, Arab, Norman, Spanish and German cultures, which has resulted in the emergence of a genuinely local cultural quality. The Cappella Palatina (12th century) in the Palazzo Reale of the Sicilian city Palermo is perhaps the best example of this cultural *mixis*, as it combines Norman (Latin), Arab, and Byzantine art styles. The technique of mosaics, the figure of the Christ *Pantokrator* in the apex, and the use of gold are Byzantine; the content of the mosaics of the walls (the story of the Apostle Paul) is nothing other than the Western *Biblia pauperum*; and the floral and geometrical ornaments are of Arabic origin. Similar examples of cultural syntheses can be found in Central Europe as well: The Chapel of the Holy Trinity (14th-15th century) in Lublin (south-eastern Poland) is a unique case of a Gothic building with Ruthenian-Byzantine

---

[8] The Great Moravian Empire (or Great Moravia or the Moravian State) was indeed baptized within the Christian mission from Constantinople in the 9th century. However, since the empire ceased to exist quite quickly and the influence of Christianity in the Eastern rite church was very limited (Hungary, Bohemia, and Poland were all baptized again in the 10th century, this time in the Latin rite), its presence in the local heritage is minimal. See: Oskar Halecki, *Jadwiga of Anjou and the Rise of East Central Europe* (Boulder, Col.: Social Science Monographs, 1991) 4–6; Oskar Halecki, *Borderlands of Western Civilization: A History of East Central Europe* (New York: Ronald Press Company, 1952) 25–30.

[9] Halecki, *Borderlands of Western Civilization*, 85–6; 126–31; 160–8; 197–201.

frescos on the walls, and the most venerated Polish Catholic icon, the Black Madonna of Częstochowa (14th century), is in fact an Eastern Christian *Hodegetria*.

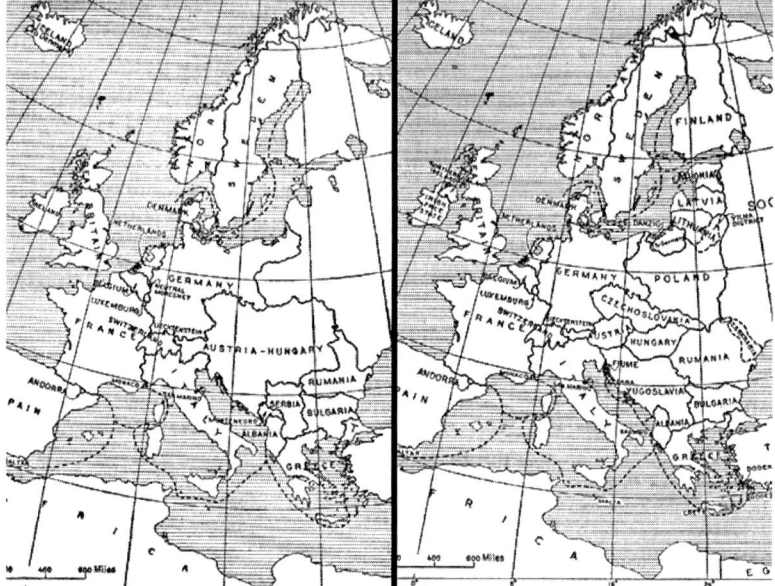

Figure 4: Europe in 1914 and in 1924. Public Domain.

Another important reason to distinguish Central from Eastern Europe is their different postwar histories. Putting the cases of Ukraine and Belarus aside, none of the Central European countries were a Soviet Republic prior to the Second World War, and due to this none of them experienced the prewar terror of purges, artificially created famine, or forceful collectivization. This changed following the Second World War, as the Soviet victory allowed Moscow to annex the Baltic states, Bessarabia, western Ukraine and Belarus, while satellite communist governments were established across the region. Nevertheless, this model of 'indirect rule' meant that most of the region remained outside of the USSR, and local regimes sought a modicum of accommodation with societies under their rule, which created a wider sphere of political autonomy than was possible in the Soviet Union. Poland, Czechoslovakia, Hungary, and—following its break with Moscow—Yugoslavia were able to use more lenient policies, especially salient in the sphere of culture, which had a profound impact on morale. In the mid-1970s, Václav Havel proposed a distinction between totalitarian and post-totalitarian regimes (those where one believes in the ruling system and its ideology and those where one has become deeply disillusioned with it),[10] arguing that his native Czechoslovakia was an example of the latter. Finally, it is important to note that the collapse of communist regimes and corresponding tensions in Central Europe did not trigger any violent conflicts (the only exception, again, being Romania).[11] In contrast to the turmoil that accompanied the dismantling of the Soviet Union and especially the dissolution of Yugoslavia, postwar borders were preserved during the collapse of these regimes (e.g. the German-Polish one), and the dissolution of Czechoslovakia proceeded in a peaceful and orderly fashion.

---

[10] Václav Havel, "The Power of the Powerless," in *The Power of the Powerless: Citizens against the State in Central-Eastern Europe* (London: Hutchinson, 1985) 24–96.

[11] Thus the neologism 'refolution' (a combination of 'reform' and 'revolution') proposed by Timothy Garton Ash: Timothy Garton Ash, *The Magic Lantern: The Revolution of '89 Witnessed in Warsaw, Budapest, Berlin, and Prague* (New York: Random House, 1990) 14.

Figure 5: Frescos of the Holy Trinity Chapel in Lublin (14th century). Public Domain.

Considering the period between the late 1980s and the beginning of the 21st century, one can try to distinguish three post-communist narratives: in the post-Soviet realm, the *devyanostiye* (1990s) are synonymous with corruption, economic crisis, criminality, and an overwhelming feeling of humiliation; in South-Eastern Europe, the fall of communism is associated with war, expulsions, rapes, and ethnic cleansings; and, conversely, for Central Europeans, the end of communism meant modernisation (in the spheres of economics, politics, and culture) that was both unusually rapid and astonishingly successful, even though many of its elements from today's perspective might be seen as inept or even regrettable (it is not without reason that the word 'improvisation' is frequently used to describe the post-communist era in Poland or Hungary). The later access to the European Union (EU) broadened the set of rights with such privileges as participation in the free movement of goods, capital, services, and people.[12] If, as it has been suggested, 'Central Europe' can be described with the German term *Schicksalsgemeinschaft* ('the community of fate'), it must be admitted that for Central Europeans this fate (in the last years of the 20th and the first of the 21st century) was much more fortunate than for people in many other parts of the world.

*

---

[12] The case of Ukraine is more complex, as this country experienced most of the trauma entailed by the fall of the USRR, and what is more, the nuclear catastrophe in Chernobyl (1986). In the sphere of culture, however, one could observe similar tendencies as in Poland or Czechia: first and foremost the revival of local (e.g. Galician) identities and traditions, which allows Ukraine to be placed in a line of continuity with its Western neighbours.

Figure 6: Europe between Hitler and Stalin: military parade held by the troops of Nazi Germany and the Soviet Union in Brest-Litovsk (September 1939). Public Domain.

When analysing Ukrainian, Polish or German literature of the past twenty-thirty years, one notices many elements of spatiotemporal fluctuations. In this context, the notion of 'Central Europe' turns out to be highly useful thanks to its potential of cultural inclusion and conceptual transformability. While old borders were disappearing and new borders were being set, new topics and discourses appeared; questions concerning ethnic / national or sexual minorities and challenging issues from the past (e.g. local responsibility for the Shoah) were being raised. During this time, various forms of *Reiseliteratur*—travel literature, a hybrid genre combing narrative, essay, and literary diary—were mastered by such authors as Yurii Andrukhovych, Ziemowit Szczerek, Martin Pollack, and Andrzej Stasiuk. The spatial narratives of Central Europe started to treat space as a multicultural palimpsest, broaching issues that could not have been mentioned before. In such narratives, one can find elements of uncertainty following 'being in transfer' and various forms of nostalgia. On the other hand, the predominant conviction in these narratives is that this period of time was the 'end of history,' which allowed for distance, irony, and an exploration of private and local themes—tendencies which have been sharpened still further by the appearance of capitalism and mass culture. It was even possible to treat the experience of living in a cemetery, in the former 'bloodlands,'[13] as a source of humour. In his short text *The Decalogue of a True European* the Polish writer Jerzy Pilch describes the fate of his native Cieszyn Silesia (nowadays the borderland of Czechia and Poland) in the following way:

> My grandma, for the whole of the 20th century, never left the house, and despite this sluggishness (or maybe thanks to it), she was in turn a citizen of k.u.k. Austria-Hungary, Czech[oslovakia] (twice), the Second Polish Republic, Nazi Germany, the Polish People's Republic, and the Third Polish Republic. She fell asleep in Poland and woke up in Germany; the border with Czech[oslovakia] that two days ago had gone along the mountain, clinging to our house, now went through a bridge lying fifty metres away and—after closer investigation—turned out to be a border with Poland. My grandma never travelled abroad; it was the frontiers of various countries and European powers that used to fly over the roof of our cottage as only they

---

[13] Timothy Snyder, *Bloodlands: Europe between Hitler and Stalin* (New York: Basic Books, 2010).

wanted to. To all household members the European experience was given more than to anyone else.[14]

In summary, while following the Stendhalian metaphor of the novel as a 'mirror carried along a high road,' one can say that Central European spatial narratives of the last 30 years can be compared with a mirror on which one can simultaneously see the present and the past, illuminated from different perspectives.

Figure 7: The birth of Solidarność in Poland: the Gdańsk Agreement at the Lenin Shipyard in August 1980 (graffiti in Gdańsk, 2011). Public Domain.

*

The following volume consists of four studies. The first discusses the notion of 'Central Europe' in Milan Kundera's literary and non-literary writings. The two studies following both provide a closer exploration of literary Galicia, as this region exemplifies almost all issues concerning Central Europe as an imagined space. That is, Galicia is nowadays split between the EU and non-EU, between its Habsburg and its Soviet past, between its Latin and its Orthodox heritage. Such heterogeneity (not to mention the

---

[14] Jerzy Pilch, *Dziennik* (Warszawa: Wielka Litera, 2012) 100–1. My translation.

variety of languages and dialects spoken in the region) on the one hand prohibits the emergence of one common 'Galician narrative' or 'Galician identity,' but paradoxically, it has also helped to establish a contemporary myth of 'literary Galicia;' visible in the space of disappearing and reappearing borders and states are leitmotivs in the nostalgic-ironic prose of Andrzej Stasiuk and Yurii Andrukhovych. The fourth and final article illustrates the complexity of the question of imagined Central European geographies through a discussion of nostalgia.

The main aim of the following book is to examine how the complex concept of 'Central Europe' has evolved, and to present different perspectives on literary topics. Though the main approach of the volume project was archaeological, with 2014 as a closing point, spatial narratives were also interpreted as a social commentary of possible worlds to come.

Bibliography

Barta, Peter I., ed. *Fall of the Iron Curtain and the Culture of Europe*. New York, NY: Routledge 2015.

Bauman, Zygmunt, "Intellectuals in East-Central Europe: Continuity and Change." in *In Search of Central Europe*, ed. George Schöpflin and Nancy Wood. Cambridge: Polity Press 1989, 70–90.

Brodsky, Joseph, "Why Milan Kundera Is Wrong About Dostoyevsky." *The New York Times*, February 17 (1985). http://www.nytimes.com/books/00/09/17/specials/brodsky-kundera.html (acc.11.03.2017).

Garton Ash, Timothy, "Does Central Europe Exist?" in *In Search of Central Europe*. ed. George Schöpflin and Nancy Wood, Cambridge: Polity Press 1989, 191–215.

Garton Ash, Timothy, *The Magic Lantern: The Revolution of '89 Witnessed in Warsaw, Budapest, Berlin, and Prague*. New York: Random House 1990.

Halecki, Oskar. *Borderlands of Western Civilization: A History of East Central Europe*. New York: Ronald Press Company 1952.

Halecki, Oskar. *Jadwiga of Anjou and the Rise of East Central Europe.* Boulder, Col.: Social Science Monographs 1991.

Havel, Václav, "The Power of the Powerless." in *The Power of the Powerless: Citizens against the State in Central-Eastern Europe, Contemporary politics, Václav Havel.* London: Hutchinson 1985, 24–96.

Havel, Václav. *The Power of the Powerless: Citizens against the State in Central-Eastern Europe. Contemporary politics.* London: Hutchinson, 1985.

Horel, Catherine, "The Rediscovery of Central Europe in the 1980s." in *Fall of the Iron Curtain and the Culture of Europe.* ed. Peter I. Barta. New York, NY: Routledge 2015, 24–39.

Judt, Tony, "The Dilemmas of Dissidence: The Politics of Opposition in East-Central Europe." *East European Politics & Societies* 2, no. 2 (1988): 185–240.

Judt, Tony, and Timothy Snyder. *Thinking the Twentieth Century.* New York, NY: Penguin Press 2013.

Kundera, Milan, "The Tragedy of Central Europe." *The New York Review of Books*, no. 31 (1984): 33–37. https://is.muni.cz/el/1423/jaro 2016/MEB404/um/Kundera_1984.pdf (acc. 6.10.2017).

Neumann, Friedrich. *Mitteleuropa.* Berlin: Reimer 1916. https://archive.org/stream/mitteleuropa00naumuoft (acc. 11.03.2017).

Neumann, Iver B. *Uses of the Other: "The East" in European Identity Formation.* Minneapolis: University of Minnesota Press 1999.

Pilch, Jerzy. *Dziennik.* Warszawa: Wielka Litera 2012.

Schöpflin, George and Nancy Wood, ed. *In Search of Central Europe.* Cambridge: Polity Press 1989.

Snyder, Timothy. *Bloodlands: Europe between Hitler and Stalin.* New York: Basic Books 2010.

Todorova, Marija Nikolaeva. *Imagining the Balkans.* Updated ed. Oxford: Oxford University Press 2009.

Ugrešić, Dubravka. *Fording the Stream of Consciousness.* London: Virago, 1991.

Ugrešić, Dubravka, "GW, the Gloomy Writer." in *Thank you For Not Reading: Essays on Literary Trivia*, Normal, IL: Dalkey Archive Press 2003, 105–9.

Ugrešić, Dubravka, *Thank you For Not Reading: Essays on Literary Trivia*. Normal, IL: Dalkey Archive Press 2003.

Figure 8: LGBT+ campaign *Niech nas zobaczą* in Poland (2003). Public Domain.

Iris Llop
Universitat de Barcelona, Spain

A NARRATIVE CONSTRUCTION: THE IDEA OF CENTRAL EUROPE IN MILAN KUNDERA'S WRITINGS

> Whether he is nationalist or cosmopolitan, rooted or uprooted, a European is profoundly conditioned by his relation to his homeland; the national problematic is probably more complex, more grave in Europe than elsewhere, but in any case it is different there.[1]
>
> Milan Kundera

I.

When we approach the idea of Central Europe in Milan Kundera's work, the most controversial essay is clearly *The Tragedy of Central Europe*.[2] Primarily well-known due to its publication in *The New York Review of Books* in 1984 and, secondly, because it is one of the most quoted texts from Kundera and because of the different responses from writers and intellectuals that made it the starting point of a debate about the existence and nature of a Central European identity. *The Tragedy of Central Europe* was one of Kundera's first attempts to elaborate his idea of Central Europe and it has been referenced since its publication by different studies from

---

[1] Milan Kundera, *The Curtain* (New York: Harper Collins, 2006), 31.
[2] Milan Kundera, "The Tragedy of Central Europe," *New York Review of Books* (pre-1986), April 26, 1984, 31; "Un occident kidnappé ou la tragédie de l'Europe centrale," *Le Débat* 27, no. 5 (1983): 3–23.

the Postcolonial Comparative Literature regarding Central European literature,[3] to the specialized critics of Kundera's novels,[4] such as Maria Nemcova Banerjee,[5] Fred Misurella[6] or, more recently, Martine Boyer-Weinmann.[7]

Many of these studies only take into consideration this famous article though. While it can be an interesting analysis, focused on a concrete historical and political debate, it does not give a complete portrait of Kundera's notion of Central Europe. Thus, this article cannot only be based on this only notion, since Kundera's idea of Central Europe is rewritten in several essays throughout the author's life; from the first short articles and interviews, to the literary representations of this identity in novels like *The Unbearable Lightness of Being* (1984), along with literary essays *L'art du roman* (1986), *Les testaments trahis* (1997), and *Le rideau* (2005). I will analyse the evolution of the phrasing of the idea of Central Europe in these different genres, comparing the different texts in which the Czech novelist tackles the question of Central European identity, in order to examine its evolution and to understand the reasons behind the rewriting process, especially since, as Michelle Woods has observed,

> Rewriting is not an afterthought for Kundera, it is a modus operandi. [...] It is important to analyse the interaction between these different forms of rewriting, not only because, seen together, they show a certain pathology of rewriting, but also because focusing on one form would recount only a part of the story.[8]

---

[3] Leonidas Donskis, ed., *Yet Another Europe after 1984* (Amsterdam: Editions Rodopi, 2012). Interdisciplinary comparative approaches to this text can be found in this volume.

[4] Marie-Odile Thirovin and Martine Boyer-Weinmann, eds., *Désaccords Parfaits. La réception paradoxale de l'oeuvre de Milan Kundera* (Grenoble: Ellug, 2009).

[5] Maria Nemcova Banerjee, *Terminal Paradox. The Novels of Milan Kundera* (New York: Grove Weidenfeld, 1990).

[6] Fred Misurella, *Understanding Milan Kundera. Public Events Private Affairs* (Columbia: University of South Carolina, 1993).

[7] 'Culturellement, émotionnellement et par choix assumé, Milan Kundera est un homme d'Europe centrale. Si cette notion émerge dans son discours de façon de plus en plus nette dans les années 1980, c'est qu'il la sent incomprise à l'Ouest.' Martine Boyer-Weinmann, *Lire Milan Kundera* (Paris: Armand Colin. Kindle Edition, 2009), «Ciel étoilé de l'Europe centrale» Kindle Locations, 172–174.

[8] Michelle Woods, *Translating Milan Kundera* (London: Multilingual Matters Ltd, 2006), 62.

According to the Czech semiotic and literary theory scholar Ladislav Matějka, 'the identity of Central Europe has been a problem for Milan Kundera since his adolescence; it gave birth to a theme with many variations'.[9] The firsts texts that Matějka analyses, such as *Czech destiny* or Kundera's speech at the Czech writers' convention,[10] are concerned with the specific situation of his home country, and although they contain some reflections on the context of the Czechoslovakia and the importance of small nations in the construction of the idea of Europe,[11] these arguments are still part of a national debate.[12] The term used by Matějka to describe Kundera's different versions of Central Europe gives a hint of how these various texts can be analysed, since it is a concept that Kundera inherits from his music studies and with which he elaborates his own poetic discourse about the novel.

> All that holds them [independent compositions] together, that makes them a novel, is that they treat the same themes. As I worked I thus came across another old strategy: *Beethoven's variation strategy*, this allowed me to stay in direct, uninterrupted contact with some existential questions that fascinate me and that this novel in variation form explores from multiple angles in sequence.[13]

---

[9] Ladislav Matějka, "Milan Kundera's Central Europe," *Cross Currents*, Vol. 9 (1990): 127.

[10] See Kundera's speech made at the Fourth Congress of the Czechoslovak Writers' Union, 27–29 June 1967, in Dušan Hamšík, *Writers against Rulers* (London: Hutchison, 1971). Martin Rizek analyses the context of this contribution in "Kundera l'homme politique: le discoursau IVe congrès des écrivains" in Rizek, *Comment devient-on Kundera?* (Paris: L'Harmattan – Kindle Edition, 2001).

[11] 'I believe in the great historical calling of small nations in a world that is at the mercy of great powers yearning to smooth its edges and readjust its dimensions. Because they are constantly searching for and creating their own visage, because they must struggle for their independence, small nations are the agents of resistance against the frightful influences of global uniformity, protectors of the variegation of traditions and ways of life, and guarantors that the original, the extraordinary and the idiosyncratic are at home in the world.' Milan Kundera 'Český úděl', *Listy* 7–8 (1968): 1–5. 'Czech Destiny', trans. by Tim West. https://www.academia.edu/2503513/Czech_Destiny_Milan_Kundera_ (acc. 19.12.2015).

[12] For more information about the debate between Milan Kundera and Václav Havel see: Tim West, "Destiny as Alibi: Milan Kundera, Václav Havel and the 'Czech Question' after 1968," *The Slavonic and East European Review* 87, no. 3 (2009): 401–428; Charles Sabatos, "Criticism and Destiny: Kundera and Havel on the Legacy of 1968," *Europe-Asia Studies* 60 num. 10 (2008): 1827–1845.

[13] Milan Kundera, *Testaments Betrayed* (New York, Harper Perennial – E-Book Edition, 1995), 168.

The notion of 'variation' emphasizes, like in the musical sense of the word, both the changes from one construction of the idea to the next one, but also the relation between the 'themes' and 'motifs' that these different variations have in common.

My proposal is then to study the texts in which Kundera has outlined his thoughts about Central Europe since the 1980s in order to describe a progressive transition from a discourse where the political and ideological ideas have been read as dominant to a literary discourse, by analysing the narrative construction of these ideas and their relation with Kundera's conception of what he calls 'novelistic meditation.'

Furthermore, I would also like present that, although these articles and interviews helped Kundera to make his case in the French (and I would add Western) literary field as Martin Rizek says,[14] they can be analysed as the origin of the later literary formulations of the idea of Central Europe in Kundera's narrative. Under this perspective, the notion of 'variation' understood, following Kundera own conception, as a narrative construction will be crucial to understand the relation between the different texts.

---

[14] 'Le texte le plus important pour la naissance du mythe de l'Europe centrale chez Kundera est certainement 'Un Occident kidnappé ou la tragédie de l'Europe centrale', publié en 1983 dans le numéro 27 du Débat. Nous employons le terme de mythe pour souligner le caractère imaginaire de l'Europe centrale dont les coordonnées, purement discursives, sont en grande partie déterminées par la position de Kundera dans le champ littéraire français' Rizek, *Comment devient-on Kundera?* "2ème Partie: Paratextes Chapitre VI Chantre de l'Europe centrale" Locations 1774–1777.

Figure 9: Prague Spring (1968). Public Domain.

II.

After the Soviet invasion of Czechoslovakia in 1968, Kundera's work was no longer published in his home country and all his books were removed from public libraries. Some of his novels, like *Life is Elsewhere* (1973), appeared in French translation while he was still in Prague. In 1975 Kundera and his wife emigrated to France, where the Czech writer had been invited to teach at the University of Rennes. In 1979 he moved to Paris and started to teach in l'École des Hautes Études en Sciences Sociales, the same year he was stripped of his Czechoslovak citizenship. In 1981 he became a French citizen.

For Kundera, one of the difficulties he faced as he worked his way into the French literary field was that he was often labelled as a dissident and listed next to other Russian emigrants, as he explains in *The Curtain*.[15]

---

[15] 'Nothing beats an argument from personal experience: in the late 1970s, I was sent the manuscript of a foreword written for one of my novels by an eminent Slavist, who placed me in permanent comparison (flattering, of course; at the time, no one meant me harm) with Dostoyevsky, Gogol, Bunin, Pasternak, Mandelstam, and the Russian dissidents. In alarm, I stopped its publication. Not that I felt any antipathy for Russians; on

After his emigration in 1975 to France, the Czech writer tried to explain the reasons for his departure and the reality of the Central European countries under the influence and the power of the USSR, usually facing misunderstanding and deception. As he states, "Gradually I understood that I came from a 'far-away country of which we know little'. The people around me placed great importance on politics but knew almost nothing about geography: they saw us as 'communized', not 'taken over'."[16]

The experience of being regarded as a 'man from the East' or 'an East European émigré,' is one of the factors that triggered the first public elaboration of his idea of Central Europe.

Kundera's contributions to this idea though, as Petr. A. Bílek[17] pointed out, were part of a larger debate lead by Central European writers such as Danilo Kiš,[18] Czesław Miłosz[19] or György Konrád,[20] that had suffered the experience of exile and that raised the question of Central European identity in the eighties with their articles, essays and interviews. These different contributions characterized the idea of Central Europe as a 'Theme' a 'Dream' or several 'Attitudes,' that is, not in conflictive geographical terms, but in cultural images or conceptions of what united Central European people. Some of them, such as Konrád's text presented a project[21] more than a concrete reality, a possibility against the nationalist constructions of identity that had led to conflicts and to the Cold War period. Others, like Kiš, raised more questions than answers about the entity of Central

---

the contrary, I admired them all, but in their company I became a different person.' Milan Kundera, *The Curtain*, 36.

[16] Ibid.
[17] Petr. A. Bílek, "Littérature tchèque, littérature centre-centre européenne et littérature mondiale dans l'oeuvre essayistique de Milan Kundera" in *Désaccords Parfaits. La réception paradoxale de l'oeuvre de Milan Kundera*, 37–48.
[18] Danilo Kiš, "Variations on the Theme of Central Europe," *Cross Currents* 6 (1987): 1–14. A study of Kiš' idea of Central Europe can be found in Vladimir Zoric, "The mirror and the map: Central Europe in the late prose of Danilo Kiš," *Knjizevna istorija* 46, no. 153 (2014): 505–524.
[19] Czesław Miłosz, "Central European Attitudes," *Cross Currents* 5 (1986): 101–108.
[20] György Konrád, "Is the Dream of Central Europeu Still Alive?" *Cross Currents* 5 (1986): 109–12.
[21] 'The Central European idea can be considered a perverse fantasy, but its singularity lies in the fact that many Central Europeans need a horizon of that kind, so much broader than of the national state.' Konrád, "Is the Dream of Central Europe Still Alive?" 121.

Europe, but all those texts expressed a shared belief in culture and, especially in literature, as the cornerstone of that identity.

Similar formulations of this identity can be found in the conversation that the American novelist Philip Roth had in 1980 with Milan Kundera. The interview was published in *The New York Times* under the title *The Most Original Book of the Season*. Some critics like Martin Rizek may regard this text as a presentation of Kundera to the Anglophone public and by this, to the Western readers, but I would like to read it as well as one of the first contributions to the Central European debate that Bilek has described. When asked about the relation between Eastern and Western Europe, the Czech author attempts a definition of Central Europe:

> As a concept of cultural history, Eastern Europe is Russia, with its quite specific history anchored in the Byzantine world. Bohemia, Poland, Hungary, just like Austria have never been part of Eastern Europe. From the very beginning they have taken part in the great adventure of Western civilization, with its Gothic, its Renaissance, its Reformation—a movement which has its cradle precisely in this region. It was here, in Central Europe, that modern culture found its greatest impulses; psychoanalysis, structuralism, dodecaphony, Bartok's music, Kafka's and Musil's new aesthetics of the novel. The post-war annexation of Central Europe (or at least its major part) by Russian civilization caused Western culture to lose its vital centre of gravity. It is the most significant event in the history of the West in our century, and we cannot dismiss the possibility that the end of Central Europe marked the beginning of the end for Europe as a whole.[22]

For Kundera, the perception of Central Europe as part of the Eastern world, which he associates with Russian civilization, results from the division of the continent after World War II. He considers that, until that moment, the countries that made up Central Europe had shared the same cultural history and tradition as the rest of Western Europe. Continuing that argument, the specificity of Central Europe lies in the cultural bonds connecting it with the other Western European nations, and in its contributions to different artistic traditions, such as literature, music or even philosophy.

The cultural bonds are reflected as well in his own ideas of the novel and the literary tradition that he presents to the Western public. That is

---

[22] Philip Roth, "The Most Original Book of the Season", *The New York Times*, November 30, 1980, https://www.nytimes.com/books/98/05/17/specials/kundera-roth.html (acc. 15.12.2015).

why I describe his sketch of Central Europe—defined by a cultural tradition and not exactly by political borders—as the literary and cultural context with which he wants to be related. Rizek argues though that this construction has an ulterior objective, which is to intervene in the reception of Kundera's work and avoid a political reception of his novels, benefiting from the Western ignorance of the Central European context.

> La défense kundérienne de l'Europe centrale est toujours aussi une défense de sa propre oeuvre qu'il aimerait soustraire au cadre historique et politique d'après-guerre. Dans cet effort, il ne reculera pas toujours devant des affirmations à l'emporte-pièce, parfois très tendancieuses que d'autres représentants de la région ou des intellectuels occidentaux contesteront.[23]

Although Rizek's argument can be part of Kundera's strategy, it is important to bear in mind that as Jørn Boisen says, despite his influence on the first academic reception of his work with his articles and paratexts, he aims to avoid political interpretation of his novels, such as what happened with *The Joke* (1967).

> Il n'y a rien dans ces préfaces qui dicte au lecteur ou à la critique comment il faut comprendre le roman, rien qui impose une certaine lecture du message du livre. Il y a en revanche une tentative beaucoup plus modeste de mettre en avant une manière de lire, qui n'enferme pas le roman dans la seule dimension politique, mais qui reste ouverte à l'indétermination de l'univers romanesque et sensible à sa dimension esthétique.[24]

In 1982 Kundera was interviewed by Alain Finkielkraut and he spoke freely about the Prague Spring and about the effects that this cultural revolution had on the French perception of Central Europe and the cultural and political debates that it raised between French intellectuals.

Although the conversation centres mainly on Kundera's opinions on Czech politics and his own novels, at the end of the interview the novelist introduces one of the arguments that he will present in *The Tragedy of Central Europe* (1984). When asked about the influence of some Central European writers like Hermann Broch, Robert Musil and Franz Kafka,

---

[23] Rizek, *Comment devient-on Kundera?* "2ème Partie: Paratextes Chapitre VI Chantre de l'Europe centrale" Kindle Locations 1736–1738.

[24] Jørn Boisen, "Le malentendu – Kundera et ses paratextes," *Neohelicon* 37 (2010): 300.

Kundera acknowledges them as the source of the sceptical attitude towards political and historical discourses that he himself had defended during the conversation. To Kundera, the experience of the constant political changes in Central Europe has helped the artists of the region to develop a critical discourse towards the rhetoric of each political power. This sceptical attitude is often translated into literary pieces that reflect upon reality through fiction, a technique that he will try to develop later in his own writing.

> It is from Central Europe that a lucid form of scepticism has arisen in the midst of our era of illusions. It is a scepticism that is attributable to the experience of an extremely concentrated history: we have seen the collapse of a great empire in the course of our century, the awakening of nations, democracy, fascism, we have seen the Nazi occupation, the glimmer of socialism, massive deportations, the Stalinist reign of terror and its downfall, and finally, we have seen the most essential thing of all—the death throes of the West within our own countries and before our own eyes. This is why I am always shocked by the perfidious vocabulary that has transformed Central Europe into the East. […] Yet Central Europe no longer exists. The three wise men of Yalta split it in two and condemned it to death. They didn't give a damn about whether it was a question of a great culture or not.[25]

This form of scepticism will be also described as specifically Central European by Czesław Miłosz, who, as Petr A. Bílek remembers, described the idea of Central Europe in *The Witness of Poetry* as a cultural community based in common approaches to the world such as scepticism and a certain sense of absurd and grotesque.[26]

These last reflections bring us to *The Tragedy of Central Europe* (1984), originally published in French in *Le Débat* in 1983. This article represents a point of inflection in Kundera's exposition of his thoughts about Central Europe, not only because he no longer depends on the questions of another writer or a journalist to build his discourse, but because in it he rehearses the form that he will later develop in his literary essays and become part of what he considers his proper literary work.[27]

---

[25] Alain Finkielkraut, "Milan Kundera Interview" in *Critical Essays on Milan Kundera*, ed. Peter Petro (New York: K. Hall & Co., 1999), 44.
[26] Bílek, "Littérature tchèque, littérature centre-centre européenne et littérature mondiale dans l'oeuvre essayistique de Milan Kundera," 47.
[27] It has to be remembered that in 1990, in an author's note to a Czech edition of *The Joke*, Kundera selected from his literary and essayistic production the texts that he considered

The singularity of this text lies in its formal characteristics: the structure of the article in short numbered chapters; the alternation of passages in which he tells historical and autobiographical anecdotes as if they were part of a novel; the presence of typically essayistic general reflections; the strong voice of the author, and a large number of footnotes, a typical mark of academic writing.

This article begins with a historical event: shortly before the Russians invaded Budapest in 1956, a Hungarian news agency director sent a dispatch, the last words of which were: 'We are going to die for Hungary and for Europe.' Kundera reads in this message the strong belief that the assault of Hungary was at the same time an attack on Europe itself, due to their mutual connections. The author uses this anecdote as a point of departure for his argument, namely, that the nations behind the Iron Curtain shared a common cultural history with the countries of Western Europe, despite its 'kidnapping' by the Soviet civilization. In Kundera's words:

> As a result, three fundamental situations developed in Europe after the war: that of Western Europe, that of Eastern Europe, and, most complicated, that of the part of Europe situated geographically in the centre—culturally in the West and politically in the East.[28]

According to the Czech novelist, that situation led to several cultural revolutions during the Cold War period, like the Hungarian revolt in 1956, the Prague Spring in 1968 and the Polish revolts in 1956, 1968 and 1970, all of them followed by Russian repression and, in some cases, by the occupation of those countries. What is most significant about those uprisings is not only that they reveal the differences between Central Europe and Russia, but also that they are mainly cultural revolutions:

---

his best work. The rest of his writing was labelled as immature, incomplete, unsuccessful and, finally, circumstantial texts. *The Tragedy of Central Europe* figures on the list of his circumstantial texts.

[28] Kundera, *The Tragedy of Central Europe*, 33.

> It was Hungarian writers, in a group named after the Romantic poet Sándor Petőfi, who undertook the powerful critique that led the way to the explosion of 1956. It was the theatre, the films, the literature and philosophy that, in the years before 1968, led ultimately to the emancipation of the Prague Spring. And it was the banning of a play by Adam Mickiewicz, the greatest Polish Romantic poet, that triggered the famous revolt of Polish students in 1968. This happy marriage of culture and life, of creative achievement and popular participation, has marked the revolts of Central Europe with an inimitable beauty that will always cast a spell over those who lived through those times.[29]

Kundera emphasizes the importance of the cultural revolutions because they reveal the real unity of Central Europe, its cultural diversity and its desire to preserve such variety: 'the greatest variety in the smallest space,' as the novelist repeats in several texts.

After defining the threats that hung over Central European cultural identity, Kundera emphasizes that these nations, despite their political weakness, played an important role in the cultural development of Europe. Examples from the first part of the 20th century alone include the work of musicians like Schönberg and Mahler, the contributions by Freud and Jung to the understanding of the human mind and the revolution of the novel brought about by authors like Kafka, Musil and Broch. Regarding this cultural history, Kundera raises the question whether there really exists a region that we can call Central Europe:

> It would be senseless to try to draw its borders exactly. Central Europe is not a state: it is a culture or a fate. Its borders are imaginary and must be drawn and redrawn with each new historical situation. […] Central Europe therefore cannot be defined and determined by political frontiers (which are inauthentic, always imposed by invasions, conquests, and occupations), but by the great common situations that reassemble peoples, regroup them in ever new ways along the imaginary and ever-changing boundaries that mark a realm inhabited by the same memories, the same problems and conflicts, the same common tradition.[30]

From these words we can infer that what Kundera is trying to describe is a cultural tradition that binds together some countries in the centre of Europe and which, he claims, should be considered an essential part of Euro-

---

[29] Ibid.
[30] Ibid., 36.

pean identity. In Kundera's opinion, the tragedy of Central European tradition is that, since 1945, it has not only had to struggle constantly to survive in the face of the Soviet influence, but it has also been forgotten by Western European nations, which not so long ago had been influenced by the linguistic revolution of Czech structuralism, the changes in the novel made by Musil or Hašek, and the new musical contributions by Janáček. According to Leonidas Donskis, by pointing this out, Kundera also wanted to highlight the lack of reflection on what defines the cultural identity of Europe.[31]

This essay was controversial not only because it accused Western Europe of forgetting the bonds it had with Central Europe but also because 'whereas Kundera described Central Europe as the embodiment of diversity within a small territory, he presented Eastern Europe as just another name for uniformity within a vast territory'.[32] However, as Stefano Bianchini observes, the writing of the article and the reactions to Kundera's article were strongly determined by Cold War patterns, and although Kundera himself was participating in a political debate, it must be remembered that the real aim of this text was not to attack other regions, but to explain the characteristics of Central Europe.[33] The value of the diversity of Central Europe, the conception of it as a paradigm of how to live with such variety of religions, languages and diasporas, is the main point of Kundera's defence of this multiple identity.

In the same year of the appearance of this article, Kundera published *The Unbearable Lightness of Being* (1984), which can be read as one of Kundera's narrative constructions of the Central European identity. In this novel he develops some reflections about the experience of exile, the conflict between cultural or personal affinities and the political borders, as well as the problems of elaborating collective memory through the different plot lines and characters in the novel.

---

[31] Donskis, "I remember, therefore I am: Milan Kundera and the Idea of Central Europe" in *Yet Another Europe after 1984*, 45.
[32] Ibid.
[33] Bianchini, "*Central Europe and Interculturality: A New Paradigm for European Union Integration?*" in *Yet Another Europe after 1984*, Donskis, 110.

The events narrated in the novel resemble some of Kundera's experiences after the Prague Spring and recreates a sort of collective memory of those who have lived through communist regimes and exile, not only because they recognize the facts, but also because of the emotions and reflections that the characters transmit.

One of the most obvious themes of this novel is the experience of exile and its different forms. Sabina, the artist, flees to Switzerland and later to the United States and never thinks about going back to the Czech Republic. Tereza and Tomáš, witnesses of the political changes that occurred in Czechoslovakia from 1968 onwards, experience the effects of history in their lives. They take part in the Prague Spring, and later Tereza reports on the Soviet invasion through photographs. Some months later they escape to Zürich; but eventually come back, partly because of the hardships of life as emigrants: the incomprehension of the Swiss neighbours, homesickness, etc. The following reflection by Tereza exemplifies that situation:

> Being in a foreign country means walking a tightrope high above the ground without the net afforded a person by the country where he has his family, colleagues, and friends, and where he can easily say what he has to say in a language he has known from childhood. In Prague she was dependent on Tomáš only when it came to the heart; here she was dependent on him for everything. What would happen to her here if he abandoned her? Would she have to live her whole life in fear of losing him?[34]

Through the novel the reader can find many passages in which the different characters express their feelings about how the exile affects their lives; for Sabina exile is constantly fleeing everything and everyone that she thinks she has betrayed, Tomáš experiences an inner exile after the frustrated physical one, and Tereza realizes her dependency on Tomáš while they are in Zürich.

The same happens with the way each character thinks about their country and their relation to words like 'nation' or 'Europe': Sabina realizes she has nothing in common with her compatriots when she attends a Czech gathering in Switzerland; this contrasts with the unreal nostalgia that the

---

[34] Kundera, *The Unbearable Lightness of Being* (New York: Harper Perennial, 1991), 75.

Swiss Franz feels towards the fate of Sabina's homeland. Through these situations and contradictions Kundera points out the impossibility of a unique form of patriotism and the singular relation of each individual with the idea of the cultural or national affinities.

All these experiences and points of view along with their reflections create a collage that tries to avoid the monological discourse (in the sense of Mikhail Bakhtin) of History. As Yvon Grenier and Velichka Ivanova[35] have pointed out, Kundera includes historical events in the novel through the filter of the character's consciousness and thus he emphasizes the complexity and plurality of the possible narratives of those historic facts. As Kundera says in *The Curtain*,

> The novel's spirit is the spirit of complexity. Every novel says to the reader: 'Things are not as simple as you think'. That is the novel's eternal truth, but it grows steadily harder to hear amid the din of easy, quick answers that come faster than the question and block it off.[36]

It is through the novel and the 'novelistic thinking'—a term which he will develop in his essays and to which I will refer later—that Kundera achieves a description of the Central European identity not only as a political or cultural idea, but as a narrative construction that can be rewritten in many variations as it continues changing, through the different points of view of the characters.

III.

As we have seen so far, the idea of Central Europe that Kundera outlines and rewrites in his articles, prologue and the two interviews allows him to make his own literary work, his roots and his cultural influences understandable for the French and Western European public. These texts, which work as paratext to the novels, could be read as a preparation of his own

---

[35] See Velichka Ivanova, "Roman versus Politique chez Milan Kundera," in *Roman & Politique. Que peut la littérature?* (Paris: Presses Universitaires de Rennes, 2009): 353–362; Velichka Ivanova, "Literature in the 'Other' Europe Before and After the Transition: The Work of Blaga Dimitrova and Milan Kundera," *Journal of Contemporary Central and Eastern Europe* 18, no. 2 (2010): 205–221.

[36] Kundera, *The Curtain*, 18.

literary reception as an emigrant writer, first in France and later in the other countries where his novels, through the translations, had become popular.

These texts also have another function in Kundera's literary work, as I have said, and I would like to suggest that they are variations of an idea that was developed in *The Unbearable Lightness of Being* and would be explored later in his literary essays. In short, I argue that the reflections found in the texts from the 1980s, and which could initially be read as circumstantial, became part of the writing process of the essay volumes and his literary writing.

Kundera's first collection of literary essays published in a volume was *The Art of the Novel* (1986). Most of the chapters of this book are articles, interviews and speeches which appeared between 1979 and 1985, but were rewritten for this book, as noticed if compared to the original texts. Thus, when the topic of Central Europe appears in this book it is related either to the novelistic tradition that Kundera describes as his pléiade (Broch, Hašek, Kafka and Musil), or to a cultural reflection on Europe. In both cases the idea of Central Europe has been integrated into a cultural context and the discourse focuses on how literature and especially the novel can create a parallel narration that contrasts with the historical, political or ideological one.

The sixth chapter of the book, *Sixty-three words*, serves as an example of a different approach to the idea of Central Europe: in it, the writer offers sixty-five definitions of words which he considers important to understand his literary work. In his definition of Central Europe, he explains how the Central European writers like Kafka, Hašek, Musil, Broch and Gombrowicz incarnate attitudes such as a 'mistrust of History' and a 'rational and demystifying lucidity' that can be traced in their essays and novels.[37]

The decision to avoid the direct political debate is clearly explained in the seventh chapter, *The Novel and Europe*, a transcription of his Jerusalem Prize acceptance speech at the Hebrew University of Jerusalem, in the spring of 1985, in which he manifested his attitude towards politics:

---

[37] Milan Kundera, *The Art of the Novel* (London: Faber & Faber, 1988), 164.

And precisely in this time of undeclared and permanent war, and in this city with its dramatic and cruel destiny, I have determined to speak only of the novel. You may have understood that this is not some attempt on my part to avoid the questions considered grave. For if European culture seems under threat today, if the threat from within and without hangs over what is most precious about it—its respect for the individual, for his original thought, and for his right to an inviolable private life—then, I believe, that precious essence of the European spirit is being held safe as in a treasure chest inside the history of the novel, the wisdom of the novel.[38]

Kundera contributes to the European debate by developing his reflections on the theory of the novel and the different narrative strategies through which this genre could have an impact on reality. He intends to do this through a novelistic reflection on Central European identity. He still has a voice in the political debate but he assumes it through an aesthetic responsibility, as the Canadian political scholar Yvon Grenier explains:

In contrast with many intellectuals of his generation, Kundera eschews the idea of political responsibility of the writer, opting instead for the aesthetic responsibility of the novelists to espouse and transmit a certain literary tradition. […] His essays on the mission of the novel seem written to defend the novel and what it represents (culture, civilization, wisdom, autonomy) against what he sees as the reductive world of ideology.[39]

Instead of writing articles and giving his opinion on interviews, Kundera describes his idea of the Central European identity through another literary genre and another form of language: the novel. The novel allows the Czech author to develop his ideas in a form of experimental thinking that he calls 'specifically novelistic essay' or 'novelistic thinking,'[40] a way of thinking that he learns from two of his admired Central European writers:

---

[38] Ibid.
[39] Yves Grenier, "Milan Kundera on Politics and the Novel," *History of Intellectual Culture* 6 (2006), 3.
[40] The notion of 'meditation romanesque' (novelistic thinking as it appears in the English translation) is developed gradually in the literary essays by Kundera and several definitions and examples of this idea can be found in the essays of the Czech author. Further interpretations of this idea can be found in Kvetoslav Chvatik, *Die Fallen der Welt. Der Romancier Milan Kundera* (München: Carl Hanser Verlag, 1994); Eva Le Grand, *Kundera ou La mémoire du désir* (Montréal: Editions XYZ, 1995). A PhD thesis that explores this idea is currently being developed by myself.

novelistic thinking, as Broch and Musil brought it into the aesthetic of the modern novel, has nothing to do with the thinking of a scientist or a philosopher; I would even say it is purposely a-philosophic, even anti-philosophic, that is to say fiercely independent of any system of preconceived ideas; it does not judge; it does not proclaim truths; it questions, it marvels, it plumbs; its form is highly diverse: metaphoric, ironic, hypothetic, hyperbolic, aphoristic, droll, provocative, fanciful; and mainly it never leaves the magic circle of its characters' lives; those lives feed it and justify it.[41]

We must remember that Kundera does not use this 'novelistic thinking' with the intention of writing a historical novel, but as a way of exploring human existence in different hypothetical situations. The characters created by him are not portraits of real people but existential possibilities that he places in the contexts he is familiar with in order to explore human behaviour, as he explains in *The Art of the Novel*.[42] This 'novelistic meditation' can be conceived as a way to keep reflecting on topics like Central Europe, but this time through literature. As Jay Daniel Miniger argues in relation to Kundera's texts,

> Central European struggles necessarily involve cultural memory, in particular the kind of memory of previously existing, if fictional, cultures—of cultures often rooted in, constructed by, and remembered through works of fiction.[43]

Similar thoughts can be found in the second chapter of Kundera's essay *The Curtain* (2006). In this text, the Czech author revisits some of his ideas about Europe, the relations between big and small countries and the effects of these international unequal relationships on the construction of the his-

---

[41] Kundera, *The Curtain*, 71.
[42] 'To apprehend the self in my novels means to grasp the essence of its existential problem. To grasp its *existential code*. As I was writing *The Unbearable Lightness of Being*, I realized that the code of this or that character is made up of certain key words. For Tereza: body, soul, vertigo, weakness, idyll, Paradise. For Tomas: lightness, weight.' Kundera, *The Art of the Novel*, 29.
[43] Jay D. Miniger, "Kundera, Nádas, and the Fiction of Central Europe," in *Yet Another Europe after 1984*, Donskis, 154.

tory of European literature. The recovery of Goethe's notion of 'Weltliteratur,'[44] which he uses as a title for one of the chapters, leads him to consider the importance of the international relations between artists and thinkers, a parallel network that makes the development of the different art disciplines possible. The diversity that this cultural network gives rise to is, according to Kundera, one of the most important European values:

> All the nations of Europe are living out a common destiny, but each is living it out differently, based on its own distinct experience. This is why the history of each European art (painting, the novel, music, and so on) seems like a relay race in which the various nations pass the baton from one to the next. [...] The dynamism and long life span of the history of the European arts are inconceivable without the existence of all these nations whose diverse experiences constitute an inexhaustible reservoir of inspiration.[45]

Despite this first ideal picture, Kundera denounces that relations between countries are often influenced by the political power of each nation and by attitudes related to that inequality, such as provincialism. According to the writer, literary and cultural relations should be based on a common desire to create new works of art, which should then be interpreted not within a national context, but within a larger—for example European— context, in which to consider the aesthetic value of each work of art:

> Geographic distance sets the observer back from the local context and allows him to embrace the large context of world literature—the only approach that can bring out a novel's aesthetic value—that is to say, the previously unseen aspects of existence that this particular novel has managed to make clear, the novelty of form it has found.[46]

After these first reflections about Europe in the context of interpreting its art, Kundera explores the difficulties met by some artists who do not have access to that larger context, either because they come from small countries where their work is judged from a provincial point of view or because they have been placed in the wrong cultural context. The latter is precisely

---

[44] The revision of the concept of 'Weltliteratur' made by Kundera has been included in recent Comparative Literature publications such as: Theo D. Haen, César Domínguez, and Mads Rosendahl Thomsen, *World literature: a reader*. (London: Routledge, 2013).
[45] Kundera, *The Curtain*, 29.
[46] Ibid., 34.

the situation that he had described in other, earlier texts, when he explained that in the French context he was labelled as 'a man from the East,' as a result of which his work had been dissociated from its original Central European context and placed in a foreign one.[47]

The description of his personal experience allows him to introduce a further reflection about the nature of Central Europe as a sort of median context based on the cultural relations among 'a whole collection of small nations between two powers, Russia and Germany,' which had lived through 'common historical situations that brought them together, at different times, in different configurations, and with shifting, never definitive borders.'[48]

At the end of the text Kundera recalls how important the notion of Central Europe had been for him when he had moved to France and was in need of a name for the tradition that had inspired his idea of the novel:

> The notion of Central Europe came to my aid on another occasion, too, this time for reasons having nothing to do with politics; it happened when I began to marvel at the fact that the terms 'novel', 'modern art', 'modern novel', meant something other for me than for my French friends. It was not a disagreement; it was, quite modestly, the recognition of a difference between the two traditions that had shaped us.[49]

In these later essays we can see how the notion of Central Europe becomes part of Kundera's aesthetic thoughts about the novel, which seems to be one of the main interests of the Czech writer. Central Europe is then, according to Kundera, a cultural tradition based on the relations between the artists of some small countries united by their common historical struggles; it is thus a community that cannot be defined by political borders but is the result of certain shared artistic interests and cultural bonds, and that can

---

[47] 'I explained that while there is a *linguistic* unity among the Slavic nations, there is no Slavic *culture*, no Slavic *world*; that the history of the Czechs, like that of the Poles, the Slovaks, the Croats, or the Slovenes (and of course, of the Hungarians, who are not at all Slavic) is entirely Western: Gothic, Renaissance, Baroque; close contact with the Germanic world; struggle of Catholicism against the Reformation. Never anything to do with Russia, which was far off, another world.' Ibid., 41.
[48] Ibid., 43.
[49] Ibid., 45.

only be grasped in each work of art. It is a cultural tradition that will survive as long as it continues to be developed by further narrative constructions.

Through this journey across the variations of the notion of Central Europe in Kundera's writing I have tried to present the phases of the narrative construction of this idea, which has been shaped in different genres and contexts since the 1980's. As I have shown, his conception of Central Europe has been presented in his texts as a cultural background, a common historical fate and collective memory, but above all approximations, it has been characterized as an idea that needs to be rewritten, redefined by the artists that have been determined by its influence and by those, like Kundera, who are committed to the Central European heritage.

Abstract

This paper analyses the different constructions of the idea of Central Europe that can be found in the essays of Milan Kundera. Though it has been a recurrent topic in his essays since the 1980s, Kundera's approach to Central European identity gradually developed from the historical and political point of view of a writer in exile (as in *The Tragedy of Central Europe*, 1984), to become part of his literary reflections on the theory of the European novel and the vindication of the Central European literary context in the history of the novel (*L'art du roman*, 1986; *Les testaments trahis*, 1997; *Le rideau*, 2005). The examination of the literary concept of Central European identity will lead to a discussion of the specific function of literature and of the novel in the construction of cultural identities. Here, the concepts of 'novelistic meditation' and 'thinking novel,' developed by Kundera in his later essays, will be analysed as narrative strategies to represent the different aspects of Central European identity: the experience of exile, the conflict between political borders and cultural affinities, and the elaboration of collective memory.

Keywords: Central Europe, Kundera, identity, narrative construction, novel, rewriting

Bibliography

Bianchini, Stefano, "Central Europe and Interculturality: A New Paradigm for European Union Integration?" in *Yet Another Europe after 1984. Rethinking Milan Kundera and the Idea of Central Europe*, ed. Leonidas Donskis. Amsterdam: Editions Rodopi 2012, 109–120.

Boyer-Weinmann, Martine. *Lire Milan Kundera*. Paris: Armand Colin. Kindle Edition 2009.

Chvatik, Kvetoslav. *Die Fallen der Welt. Der Romancier Milan Kundera*. München: Carl Hanser Verlag 1994.

Donskis, Leonidas, "I remember, therefore I am: Milan Kundera and the Idea of Central Europe." In *Yet Another Europe after 1984. Rethinking Milan Kundera and the Idea of Central Europe*, ed. Leonidas Donskis, Amsterdam: Editions Rodopi 2012, 31–50.

Donskis, Leonidas, "Identity and Memory in Eastern and Central Europe: Tracing Czeslaw Milos and Milan Kundera," *The Romanian Journal for Baltic and Nordic Studies* 7, no. 1 (2015): 69–89.

Hamšík, Dušan. *Writers against Rulers*. London: Hutchison 1971.

Finkielkraut, Alain, "Milan Kundera Interview." in *Critical Essays on Milan Kundera*, ed. Peter Petro. New York: K. Hall & Co. 1999, 33–44.

Grenier, Yvon, "Milan Kundera on Politics and the Novel." *History of Intellectual Culture*, 6, no. 1 (2006): 1–18.

Ivanova, Velichka, "Roman versus Politique chez Milan Kundera." in *Roman & Politique. Que peut la littérature?*, Paris: Presses Universitaires de Rennes 2009, 353–362.

Ivanova, Velichka, "Literature in the 'Other' Europe Before and After the Transition: The Work of Blaga Dimitrova and Milan Kundera." *Journal of Contemporary Central and Eastern Europe* 18, no. 2 (2010): 205–221.

Kundera, Milan. "Český úděl." *Listy* 7–8 (1968): 1–5.

Kundera, Milan, "The Tragedy of Central Europe." *New York Review of Books* (pre-1986), April 26, 1984.

Kundera, Milan. *The Art of the Novel*. London: Faber & Faber, 1988.

Kundera, Milan. *Testaments Betrayed* (New York, Harper Perennial) E-Book Edition 1995.

Kundera, Milan. *The Unbearable Lightness of Being.* New York: Harper Perennial 1991.

Kundera, Milan. *The Curtain.* New York: Harper Collins 2006.

Le Grand, Eva. *Kundera ou La mémoire du désir.* Montréal: Editions XYZ 1995.

Matějka, Ladislav, "Milan Kundera's Central Europe." *Cross Currents* 9 (1990): 127–134.

Miniger, J.D., "Kundera, Nádas, and the Fiction of Central Europe." In *Yet Another Europe after 1984. Rethinking Milan Kundera and the Idea of Central Europe*, ed. Leonidas Donskis. Amsterdam: Editions Rodopi 2012, 151–170.

Misurella, Fred. *Understanding Milan Kundera. Public Events Private Affairs.* Columbia: University of South Carolina 1993.

Nemcova Banerjee, Maria. *Terminal Paradox. The Novels of Milan Kundera.* New York: Grove Weidenfeld 1990.

Pireddu, Nicoletta, "European Ulyssiads: Claudio Magris, Milan Kundera, Eric-Emmanuel Schmitt." *Comparative Literature* 67, no. 3 (2015): 267–286.

Porta, Nicolas. *Auf der Suche nach einer eigenen Identität zwischen Osten und Westen. Die Mitteleuropa-Konzeption: bei Ceslaw Milosz, Jan Patocka und Milan Kundera.* Herne: Gabriele Schäfer Verlag 2014.

Rizek, Martin. *Comment devient-on Kundera?* Paris: L'Harmattan – Kindle Edition 2001.

Roth, Philip, "The Most Original Book of the Season." *The New York Times*, November 30, 1980: http://www.nytimes.com/books/98/05/17/specials/kundera-roth.html (acc. 23.02.2018).

Sabatos, Charles, "Criticism and Destiny: Kundera and Havel on the Legacy of 1968." *Europe-Asia Studies* 60, no 10 (2008): 1827–1845.

Thirovin, Marie-Odile, Martine Boyer-Weinmann, ed. *Désaccords Parfaits. La réception paradoxale de l'oeuvre de Milan Kundera.* Grenoble: Ellug, 2009.

Tötösy de Zepetnek, Steven, ed. *Comparative Central European Culture.* Indiana: Purdue University Press 2002.

West, Tim, "Destiny as Alibi: Milan Kundera, Válcav Havel and the 'Czech Question' after 1968." *The Slavonic and East European Review* 87, no 3 (2009): 401–428.

Woods, Michele. *Translating Milan Kundera.* London: Multilingual Matters Ltd 2006.

Zelenka, Milos, "L'Europe centrale dans le contexte de la géographie littéraire et symbolique." *Recherches & Travaux*, 80 (2012): 121–140.

Jagoda Wierzejska
University of Warsaw, Poland

GALICIA: AN EASTERN OR A WESTERN LAND? REMARKS ON LOCATING THE PROVINCE IN THE FRAMEWORK OF THE EAST–WEST OPPOSITION

Between 1772 and 1918, the area of East-Central Europe that is located north of the Carpathian Mountains, was a part of the Habsburg Empire officially called the Kingdom of Galicia and Lodomeria and commonly referred to as Galicia. The province stretched across the lands seized by Austria at the expense of the Polish-Lithuanian Commonwealth in the wake of the first (1772) and the third (1795) partition thereof. Its population included (but was not limited to) Poles, Ruthenians, who became Ukrainians in the course of the nineteenth century, Jews, and Germans (including Austrians).[1] Galicia constituted the biggest province of the Danube Monarchy and its important source of military reserves and natural resources. Simultaneously, the new land distinctively differed from the rest of the state in terms of socio-political circumstances and ethno-religious reality. As the North-Eastern hinterland of the Monarchy, contiguous with Russia, it also drew interest of tsars in a way that could seriously bother the Habsburgs. Therefore, the status of Galicia within the Habsburg Empire was quite problematic character from the onset of the province's history. Even though after the Napoleonic wars and the Congress of Vienna (1815) that status seemed stabilized in terms of geopolitics, it remained prone to manipulations which were anything but ideologically neutral. Un-

---

[1] For further investigation of the issue see Paul R. Magocsi, *Galicia: A Historical Survey and Bibliographical Guide* (Toronto, Buffalo, London: University of Toronto Press, 1983), 225; Paul R. Magocsi, *A History of Ukraine* (Toronto, Buffalo, London: University of Toronto Press, 1996), 423–424; Paul R. Magocsi, "Galicia: A European Land," in *Galicia: A Multicultured Land*, ed. Christopher Hann, Paul R. Magocsi (Toronto, Buffalo, London: Toronto University Press, 2005), 7–9.

til today specific cognitive frames have been imposed on the region in order to classify knowledge about it according to particular—political rather than geographical—categories.

Iryna Vushko stated: 'In the 1830s, Lemberg [today's Lviv, the capital of Galicia—J.W.] featured only two hotels: the Hôtel de l'Europe and the Hôtel de Russie, the rather charged symbolism of this pair of names suggesting the poles of identification of nineteenth-century Galicia.'[2] Let us add that the notions of 'Europe' and 'Russia,' or more broadly, 'West' and 'East,' served as a means for conceptualization of Galicia not only when it existed as a geopolitical unit within the Habsburg Monarchy but also after World War I, that is, since the time when Galicia disappeared from maps of Europe onward.

Figure 10: The Diet of the Kingdom of Galicia and Lodomeria (German: *Landtag von Galizien*), the regional assembly of the Kingdom of Galicia and Lodomeria (19th century). Public Domain.

---

[2] Iryna Vushko, *The Politics of Cultural Retreat: Imperial Bureaucracy in Austrian Galicia 1772–1867* (New Haven, London: Yale University Press, 2015), 9–10.

When Austrian policymakers and *Kulturträger* came to the newly annexed province to impose supranational unity via Germanophone administration, education, and culture, they perceived their task as bringing Galicia closer to Europe, that is, to the West. Their endeavours notwithstanding, Galicia never became what was envisioned shortly after the annexation—a model province of the Empire, a symbol of progress—it remained a byword of backwardness, barbarism, and chaos, that is, precisely what Westerners associated with the East. On the contrary, Galicians of Polish, Ruthenian / Ukrainian, and Jewish roots, maintained vivid relationships with their compatriots living in the territories of the former Polish-Lithuanian Commonwealth annexed by Russia and Prussia, particularly beyond the border with Russia, but they scarcely shared the opinion on Eastern nature of their land. Over time, already in the nineteenth century but especially in the second half of the twentieth century, the increasing number of Galicians and former Galicians started to appreciate their (erstwhile) bonds with Vienna as a proof of belonging to the Western cultural circle.

This article analyzes the phenomenon of locating Galicia within dialectical tension between 'East' and 'West,' the concepts of heavily ideologized cultural geography. According to Edward Said, these concepts determine each other mutually, insofar as the East—or the Orient—is constructed by the Occident 'as its contrasting image.'[3] Consequently, they are correspondingly associated with opposite properties: 'backwardness' and 'development,' 'barbarism' and 'civilization,' 'order 'and 'chaos.' I discuss selected examples of locating Galicia within the said framework of the East–West dichotomous opposition, which are present in various discursive perspectives, predominantly Austrian, Polish, and Ukrainian. Focusing on these perspectives, I indicate the Enlightenment provenience of the East–West opposition and its persistence evincing itself in the way bureaucrats and settlers from outside the province, as well as Galicians themselves looked on the land. My objective is to highlight that such an opposition was predominantly used to display Galicia's putative absence

---

[3] Edward Said, *Orientalism: Western Concepts of the Orient* (New York: Pantheon Books, 1978), 1.

of culture and civilization and to justify the necessity of civilizing mission in the province, that is, the Habsburgs' political, social, and cultural engineering. Simultaneously, I want to show that the opposition in question proved to be susceptible to contrary interpretations alike and sometimes played a role of testimony of Galicia's closeness to such places as Vienna, Venice, and Trieste.

Galicia: The Slavic Orient

Initially, the Austrian authorities had no clear plan of integration of the new territorial acquisition with the rest of the Monarchy. Nevertheless, such integration was an objective of the Empress Maria Theresa's son, Joseph. Therefore, on August 26, 1772, Maria Theresa issued a resolution aimed at eliminating some of the differences between the new province and the centre. Pursuant to the resolution, the Polish nobility were compelled to stop dressing in a 'Polish manner' and the staff employed in the service of the new regime was obliged to speak German or Latin and wear French-style clothes.[4] Fulfilling those orders was supposed to prevent associations with the Polish-Lithuanian Commonwealth, on the one hand, and on the other, it constituted an effect of Enlightenment thought foregrounding the ideal of cultural mission.

Much more significant changes took place in the 1780s, after the death of the Empress and the beginning of Joseph II's sole reign. The whole monarchy then underwent wide-ranging and far-reaching reforms, which pertained to social, administrative, judicial, military, church and school matters, and were called after the name of their originator—Josephinian. The centralization of state administration institutions, the establishment of state control over the church, the partial abolishment of peasants' serfdom, on the one hand, and privileges of the nobility, on the other, in all parts of the country had revolutionary overtones. In Galicia, however, these reforms were especially palpable and intense for a couple of reasons. First,

---

[4] Hans-Christian Maner, "Włączenie Galicji do monarchii habsburskiej w XVIII wieku," in *Mit Galicji*, ed. Jacek Purchla, Wolfgang Kos et al. (Kraków: Międzynarodowe Centrum Kultury, 2014), 139–144.

local social relations, that originated from the former Polish societal circumstances and differed from those in the other parts of Central Europe, were incomprehensible and had no relevance for Austrian authorities. Second, an argument of putative *Revindication* of the Polish territories by Austria[5] facilitated the undermining of old prerogatives of the Polish noblemen and run the reforms in the region easier than in the other Habsburg lands. Third, finally, the reforms could serve as an effective means for adapting the newly acquired Eastern province to the rest of the country and opening it (the province) to the West. In the wake of the broad and strongly pushed Josephinian project, the nineteenth-century Galicia became 'a product' not only of imperial politics and complicated internal national relations, but also—according to Andriy Zayarnyuk's expression—'of social experiments of Habsburg state.'[6]

---

[5] The argument referred to the allegedly unexpired rights of the Hungarian Crown to the Principality of Galicia-Volhynia. These rights went back to the thirteenth century when the Hungarian prince Coloman became a king of Galicia. Then they were to be passed to the Habsburgs as to 'the kings of Hungary.' In 1741, Maria Teresa along with the Crown of St. Stephen took the title of 'the Queen of Galicia and Lodomeria.' In the wake of that move, in 1772, the annexation of the territory of the Polish-Lithuanian Commonwealth was made by Austria under the pretext of *Revindication* and Galicia was acclaimed as *terra recuperate*. In a similar way the rights of the Crown of Bohemia to the Duchy of Auschwitz and Zator were justified. Such a justification was fiercely criticized by different Galician milieus. In 1773, a Polish diplomat and historian, Felix Łoyko, debunked it in a text *Odpowiedź na wykład poprzedzający prawa Korony Węgierskiej do Rusi Czerwonej i Podola, tak jako Korony Czeskiej do Księstwa Oświęcimskiego i Zatorskiego*. For the further investigation of the issue see Stanisław Grodziski, *Historia ustroju społeczno-politycznego Galicji 1772–1918* (Wrocław: Zakład Narodowy im. Ossolińskich, 1971), 26–29; Stanisław Hubert, *Poglądy na prawo narodów w Polsce czasów Oświecenia* (Wrocław: Zakład Narodowy im. Ossolińskich, 1960), 207f.

[6] Andriy Zayarnyuk, "Imperium, chłopi, ruchy narodowe – galicyjski trójkąt postkolonialny?," *Historyka* 42 (2012), 101–113. See also: Larry Wolff, "Inventing Galicia: Messianic Josephinism and the Recasting of Partitioned Poland" *Slavic Review* 63, no 4 (2004), 818–840; Henryk Wereszycki, *Pod berłem Habsburgów. Zagadnienia narodowościowe* (Kraków: Wysoki Zamek, 2015), 33–46.

Figure 11: Jewish musicians from Rohatyn in Eastern Galicia (1912). Public Domain.

A 'seamless' inclusion of Galicia in the structure of the country intended by Joseph II was in fact an idea of creating a model of a new state system in a model province of the reformed Monarchy. Such an idea was in line with the spirit of enlightened absolutism and cameralism (German *Kameralismus*). Its ideological background and propulsion were both constituted by a vision of Eastern Europe as a region of multifaceted backwardness, formed in the Enlightenment and very much alive to this day. An American historian Larry Wolff explains the origins of this vision as follows:

> The issue of backwardness and development in Eastern Europe were broached and defined in the eighteenth century, not essentially as economic issues, and they continue to frame our conception of these lands. It was Eastern Europe's ambiguous location, within Europe but not fully European, that called for such notions as backwardness and development to mediate between the poles of civilization and barbarism. In fact, Eastern Europe in the eighteenth century provide Western Europe with its first model of underdevelopment, a concept that we now apply all over the world.[7]

The model described by Wolff entailed presenting Eastern Europe as a kind of non-Europe in the European bosom, a space for economic underdevelopment, as well as chaos and savagery, only waiting for *Kulturträger* from the West. Application of this idea to Galicia provided the Habsburg

---

[7] Larry Wolff, *Inventing Eastern Europe: The Map of Civilization on the Mind of the Enlightenment* (Stanford: Stanford University Press, 1994), 9.

imperial power in the province with a sense of civilizing mission. From the Austrian perspective, Galicia was backward, chaotic and savage indeed, but it was backwardness, chaos and savagery which were supposed to be set in order through reforms. That ideological framework of the Josephinism was of fundamental importance because it delivered a (new) warranty for both the reputed *Revindication* and allegedly indispensable changes which were to integrate the province with the metropolis. Unlike Maria Theresa, Joseph II did not have to justify the annexation of Polish territories referring to the questionable claims of medieval Hungary and Bohemia. As Wolff explains, he could propound a 'more modern claim to legitimacy' that emphasized the advantages of superseding Polish 'barbaric cruelty' with the Austrian 'enlightened government.'[8]

The idea of civilizing mission, that is, systematic transformation of Galicia in the spirit of the Enlightenment, found support in Germanophone literature pertaining to the region and emerging after the first partition of the Polish-Lithuanian Commonwealth, especially in the 1780s. The considerably significant development of that literature was stimulated by at least three factors. In the first decades after 1772 many German speakers came to Galicia to fill vacancies in the military, administration, and education. The German speaking audience from outside Galicia displayed interest in the new land, also as a consequence of the controversy brought about by the Josephinian reforms. What is more, the Austrian authorities, especially at the peak of the reformist offensive, needed accounts of Galicia—accounts delivered by writers-travellers who adhered the Josephinism and who would justify the imperial governance in the province.[9]

---

[8] Wolff, "Inventing Galicia," 823.
[9] The comprehensive analysis of the historical context of development of the Germanophone literature on Galicia can be found in Maria Kłańska, *Daleko od Wiednia. Galicja w oczach pisarzy niemieckojęzycznych 1772–1918* (Kraków: Universitas, 1991); Maria Kłańska, "Die deutschsprachige Literatur Galiziens und der Bukowina von 1772 bis 1945," in *Deutsche Geschichte im Osten Europas. Galizien, Bukowina, Moldau*, ed. Isabel Röskau-Rydel (Berlin: Siedler Verlag, 1999), 381–482.

The two best-known iterations of Germanophone literature about Galicia of that period were *Briefe über den itzigen Zustand von Galizien* [*Letters about the Current Situation of Galicia*][10] by Franz Kratter (1760–1838) and, conceived of as a response to Kratter's book, *Dreyssig Briefe über Galizien* [*Thirty Letters from Galicia*][11] by Alfons Heinrich Traunpaur. Kratter, a young man from Oberdorf, spent six months in Galicia, in 1784. He came to visit his brothers, wine traders in Lemberg, and was looking for a job, having applied in vain for a professorship at the Lemberg University. The collection of his impressions on Galicia, issued anonymously in Leipzig in 1786, for the first time made the province a subject of debate in the public sphere, in Galicia itself, however, the book was received as an appalling libel. After a few years Kratter returned to the region permanently and took a position of the head of the Lemberg Theatre. Before it happened, Traunpaur, a Capitan of the Austrian army coming from Habsburg Brussels, had lived in the province much longer, for eight years, therefore, he considered himself more entitled to expressing opinions on the region than the first author. In his work published also anonymously in Vienna and Leipzig at the same time, in 1787, Traunpaur accused Kratter of disseminating 'superficial remarks' on the province and opposed the disparaging depiction of the region.[12] Regardless of these differences, the publications turned out to be similar in the manner of presenting Galicia. They combined reliable information about the local life with unbelievable, though presented as true (and then disseminated), anecdotes emphasising exoticism, oddity, and wildness of the province. Both books, therefore, showed the region in the way that can be called Orientalizing.[13] The authors recognized the dynamic of imperial power and the logic of backwardness and development in Galicia, suggesting that it was

---

[10] Franz Kratter, *Briefe über den itzigen Zustand von Galizien* (Leipzig: Verlag G. Ph. Wucherers, 1786; Reprint: Berlin: Helmut Scherer Publishing House, 1990).
[11] Alphons H. Traunpaur, *Dreyssig Briefe über Galizien: oder Beobachtungen eines unpartheyischen Mannes, der sich mehr als nur ein paar Monate in diesem Königreiche umgesehen hat* (Wien, Leipzig: G. Wucherer und E. Beer, 1787; Reprint: Berlin: Helmut Scherer Publishing House, 1990).
[12] Traunpaur, *Dreyssig Briefe*, 1–4.
[13] See: E. Said, *Orientalism*.

a kind of colonial new world, 'a new Peru,'[14] to quote Traunpaur's words. Galicia seemed to the both authors a land of the boundless steppes, inaccessible Carpathian crags, wolves chasing sledges with travellers, and gloomy castles in possession of mad masters. The only group which was supposed to spread civilization in this wilderness were Germans. All the rest—smallholder and usually illiterate Ruthenian and Polish peasants, orthodox Jews and Hasids, Greek and Roman Catholic clergy, petty nobles and great Polish landowners—were imbued with barbarism. However, it was the latter, that is, the Polish gentry, who treated their surfs like slaves, who were presented as the most savage. Kratter repeatedly described a regional nobleman as 'the most inhuman, abominable barbarian' that was 'from his youth destined for unlimited command, through coarse, wild and horrible actions hardened to the point of 'tigerish' insensitivity.'[15] Traunpaur claimed to have attempted at presenting a more unbiased portrait of that estate's manners but in fact he could not refrain from repeating anecdotes on nobility's vice and violence inherent to Galicia; anecdotes that curiously corresponded with those delivered by Kratter and that aroused thrill of German speaking public: on incest, raping peasant virgins according to the *ius primae noctis*, shooting to Jews for fun etc. Ultimately, both of the writers evenly championed the outlook that only by recasting the population of the province, starting with Polish gentry, into Habsburg subjects, would make them fit into the Danube Monarchy and the civilized world permeated with Western spirit.

Publications by Kratter and Traunpaur, as well as their followers,[16] presented the image of Galicia in contrast to the rest of the state, as the Other

---

[14] Traunpaur, *Dreyssig Briefe*, 170.
[15] Kratter, *Briefe über den itzigen Zustand*, 165, 169–170.
[16] Stanisław Schnür-Pepłowski, the Polish literary historian, listed following German speaking authors who, according to him, were akin to Kratter or Traunpaur 'in terms of temperament,' that is, their attitude towards Galicia: Heinrich Gottfried Bretschneir and Joseph August Schultes, see: Schnür-Pepłowski, *Galiciana 1778–1812* (Lviv: H. Altenberg, 1897), 44–52, Schnür-Pepłowski, *Cudzoziemcy w Galicyi 1787–1841* (Kraków: Spółka Wydawnicza Polska, 1902), 1, 83–146. In *Cudzoziemcy w Galicyi* Schnür-Pepłowski added Ernst Bogumil Kortum and August Behr to the former pair of names, 39–65, 195–198. It seems reasonable to mention at least two other followers of Kratter and Traunpaur: the author of *Aus Galizien*, Wilhelm Zerboni di Sposetti and Karl Emil Franzos, who I will refer to on the following pages.

of the Monarchy. Nonetheless, they played an important role in the process of the province's integration with the new centre, having served the political objectives of the Habsburgs. The publications in question created a vision of the land of very specific qualities derived directly from the Enlightenment cultural geography. Namely, they suggested that Galicia was a distinctive Eastern territory that needed a reign of new rulers edifying those who lived in inhumane—from the Josephinian viewpoint—conditions. According to such writers as Kratter and Traunpaur, and above all, Joseph II himself, the roadmap to develop the alleged *terra recuperata* led from backwardness of the Polish-Lithuanian Commonwealth, through the progress of Galicia, to the civilization of (Western) Europe, invariably under the leadership of Austria. One can presume, however, that this path ahead was never-ending. At any rate, if the civilizing mission in Galicia had been completed, the connection with the new centre and the leadership of new rulers would have proven to be superfluous.

That ideological context of Galicia's integration with the Habsburg imperial state has had various repercussions in the history and culture of the region. Generally speaking, they have taken a form of the phenomenon under study, that is, discursive locating Galicia between antithetical categories of 'East' and 'West.' Such a trend already manifested itself at the time of the third partition, when Austria acquired new lands at the expense of the Polish-Lithuanian Commonwealth. These lands, called the New Galicia or Western Galicia, had a separate governor, Johann Wenzel Margelik, whose decisive qualification for the position was his Galician experience during Joseph II's regime. The foregoing suggested that Josephinian project was to be extended to the new broadly outlined province.[17] Austrian propaganda of that time emphasized that Western Galicia should catch up as soon as possible with the Eastern (in terms of geography) part of the land that had been flourishing under the Habsburg rule already for twenty years, and that consequently had started gaining truly Western

---

[17] See Wolff, "Inventing Galicia," 835–836; Wolff, *The Idea of Galicia: History and Fantasy in Habsburg Political Culture* (Stanford: Stanford University Press, 2010), 53–55.

character. In 1796, in Vienna, the anonymous work *Geographisch-historische Nachrichten von Westgalizien oder den neu erlangten österreichisch-polnischen Provinzen* [*Geographical-historical report on Western Galicia or the newly acquired Austrian-Polish provinces*] was brought out. It continued presenting the region in the same way as Kratter and Tranpauer had done it, only emphasising a specific asymmetry between Western and Eastern Galicia. According to the author of the publication, the new Austrian domain, having undergone a visible decay under the Polish rule, was now to experience resurrection and inevitable progress under the aegis of the Habsburgs, 'as the example of East Galicia may notably convince us.'[18]

Much later, in the 1870s and 1880s of the nineteenth century, Karl Emil Franzos (1848–1904) gave evidence of thinking in a similar way by publishing six volumes of the 'cultural images' of Galicia, Bukovina, Southern Russia, and Romania, which bore the subtitle *Aus Half-Asien* [*From Half-Asia*].[19] The author, originating from a Jewish family (but considering himself a German of Mosaic faith), was brought up in Chortkiv and educated in Chernivtsi. Then he was staying in Graz, Vienna, and from 1888 in Berlin as his political allegiance was strongly pro-Prussian. Franzos did not conceal that the *bon mot* 'Half-Asia,' revealing colonial associations, was to serve the cultural, social, and political, not topographical, characteristics of the region of his interest. He explained it in terms reminiscent of the Josephinian project of Galicia and the Enlightenment perspective on Eastern Europe as a whole. On these lands, he argued,

> European culture and Asiatic barbarism strangely encounter one another, European striving and Asiatic indolence, European humanity and such wild, such terrible conflict between nations and religious communities that it must appear to the resident of the West as not just unfamiliar but actually shocking, even unbelievable. The

---

[18] *Geographisch-historische Nachrichten von Westgalizien oder den neu erlangten österreichisch-polnischen Provinzen* (Vienna: Johann Otto, 1796), quoted after: Wolff, *The Idea of Galicia*, 54.

[19] Karl E. Franzos, *Aus Halb-Asien. Kulturbilder aus Galizien, der Bukowina, Südrussland und Rumänien* (Leipzig: Duncker & Humblot, 1876); Franzos, *Vom Don zur Donau. Neue Kulturbilder aus Halb-Asien*, (Leipzig: Duncker & Humblot, 1878); Franzos, *Aus der grossen Ebene. Neue Kulturbilder aus Halb-Asien* (Leipzig: Duncker & Humblot, 1888).

surface, the form, in these lands are in many ways borrowed from the West; the essence, the spirit are in many ways autochthonous and barbaric.[20]

Franzos characterized Eastern Europe, especially Galicia, in terms of half-Orient or Slavic Orient, that is, in the categories established since the second half of the eighteenth century, rooted much more in ideology, than in geography. The author stressed a need of the German mission to civilize in the East. According to his viewpoint, only such mission, understood in terms of an ideal cultural vocation, could help 'half-Asian' nations to rise from economic and civilizational backwardness that, in his opinion, they were still struggling with almost a century after the epoch of the Josephinian reforms.

Insofar as conceiving of Galicia in such a way was deeply grounded in Habsburg politico-cultural thought, as well as in the German public's opinion, it is not surprising that Austrian propaganda referred to it upon the fall of the province along with the Danube Monarchy, in 1918. On November 1, Poles and Ukrainians began fights of Lviv, followed by the three-day pogrom in the Jewish quarter of the city, November 21–23, and the war of Eastern Galicia which ended with the Polish victory only in mid-July 1919.[21] Viennese press wildly commented on those events having recalled such notions as the failed Habsburg civilizing mission and the collapse of the region into barbarism, worse than that of 'remote and godforsaken [...] Russian steppe.'[22] To all appearances, the argument of the need of civilizing the region, reputedly backward and barbarian, survive the fall of the Empire. A striking testimony to this argument's longevity constituted also by the fact that other, non-Austrian regimes would willingly use

---

[20] Quoted after: Carl Steiner, *Karl Emil Franzos, 1848–1904: Emancipator and Assimilationist* (New York: Peter Lang, 1990), 53–54.

[21] Thus far unrivaled monograph of the Polish-Ukrainian war is Maciej Kozłowski, *Między Sanem a Zbruczem. Walki o Lwów i Galicję Wschodnią 1918–1919* (Cracow: Znak, 1990). Particularly valuable works of the subject of the Lviv pogrom in 1918 are Alexander V. Prusin, *Nationalizing a Borderland: War, Ethnicity, and Anti-Jewish Violence in East Galicia, 1914–1920* (Tuscaloosa: University of Alabama Press, 2005), 75–91; William W. Hagen, "The Moral Economy of Popular Violence: The Pogrom in Lwów, November 1918," in *Antisemitism and its Opponents in Modern Poland,* ed. Robert Blobaum (Ithaca, London: Cornell University Press, 2005), 124–147.

[22] *Neue Freie Presse*, November 27, 1918. Quoted after: Wolff, *The Idea of Galicia*, 370.

it while seizing the land in different moments of the twentieth century. In 1918–1923, when the political status of the province was still uncertain,[23] the Polish elites sought to persuade the national and international public opinion that the province, its Ukrainian majority notwithstanding, should have been included into the Polish state; otherwise, they claimed for the sake of their interests, the land would plunge into economic and cultural devastation.[24] Surprisingly, after World War II, even the Soviet power did not restrain from taking advantage of such a reasoning. Although oblivious and hostile to the name and legacy of Galicia, it often justified its imperial moves in terms of indispensable modernization that unintentionally echoed the erstwhile rhetoric of the Habsburgs.[25]

Galicia: A Bulwark of the West

Presenting Galicia as an intermediary domain between Europe and Asia, tending to the latter pole of the East–West opposition, reached the late eighteenth century and should be understood in terms of a broader enlightened concept of the chasm between Eastern and Western Europe. During the course of the nineteenth century, however, another phenomenon started to emerge. The Austrian province was characterized within the framework of the same binary system but with a significant difference: this time Galicia was associated not with the latter but with the former pole thereof, the one connoting such notions as 'Europe,' 'development,' and 'order' rather than 'Asia,' 'backwardness,' and 'chaos.' Such a discursive

---

[23] The fate of Galicia was practically sealed by the Peace of Riga, on March 18, 1921, attributing the Eastern part of the province to the Second Polish Republic, but the Polish sovereignty on the land was internationally acknowledged only on May 15, 1923. By some Ukrainians, however, it was not accepted as legitimate.

[24] For further investigation of the issue see: Kozłowski, *Między Sanem a Zbruczem*, 271f. Christoph Mick, *Lemberg, Lwów, L'viv, 1914–1947: Violence and Ethnicity in a Contested City* (West Lafayette: Purdue University Press, 2016), especially 152–153, 174–177; Jagoda Wierzejska, "Walki polsko-ukraińskie o Lwów w literaturze dla dzieci i młodzieży dwudziestolecia międzywojennego," *Bibliotekarz Podlaski* 33, no 2 (2016), 97–118.

[25] For further investigation of the issue see: Tarik Cyril Amar, *The Paradox of Ukrainian Lviv: A Borderland City between Stalinists, Nazis, and Nationalists* (New York: Cornell University Press, 2015), 143–220.

and ideological move was made basically by the dwellers of the region themselves and aimed at appreciating Galicia as a part of allegedly more civilized world. According to that perspective, the province, instead of being presented as the Other of Europe, in general, and the Danube Monarchy, in particular, was included into their cultural borders. It should be kept in mind, however, that a need to mark the borders of belonging against a threatening Other constituted one of 'persistent geopolitical instincts of the European idea through the ages,'[26] according to the words of Michael Heffernan. This is why, concurrently with including Galicia into Europe, another Other must have been indicated: the Other which was more 'Eastern' than the province in terms of cultural geography and the one against the backdrop of whom it could seem more 'European.' The role of such an Other was attributed predominantly to Russia.

Striking proofs of adopting this perspective were delivered first by the Polish-Galician discourse in the second half of the nineteenth century. On December 10, 1866, the Galician Diet [*Sejm*], then and throughout its history dominated by Polish aristocracy and noblemen,[27] issued a famous official declaration of loyalty to the Emperor Franz Joseph I. A well-known idea of the Habsburg civilizing mission, though without references to its implementation promptly after the partitions by German speaking policy-makers and *Kulturträger*, was used there to present Galicia as an outpost, not an outcast, of the Western civilization. The deputies of the Diet, on behalf of all Galicians, declared: 'Without fear of abandoning our national idea, with faith in the mission of Austria [...] we affirm from the depths of our hearts that we stand with you, Your Majesty, and wish to stand with you.' The Majesty, that is, the Emperor was to represent the state being 'the most powerful expression of respect for freedom, and in its external

---

[26] Michael Heffernan, *The Meaning of Europe: Geography and Geopolitics* (London: Arnold, 1998), 29.
[27] See: Grodziski, *Sejm Krajowy galicyjski 1861–1914*, vol. 1 (Warsaw: Wydawnictwo Sejmowe, 1993).

organization the shield of the civilization of the West, the rights of nationality, humanity, and justice.'[28] The emphasis on the role of Austria as a protector of 'Westerness' played a particularly important role in the declaration of seemingly unconditional loyalty of Galicians. It gave rise to legitimization of the province's access to the same cultural sphere that the Danube Monarchy belonged to, as the Austrian crown land of Galicia, at least in the eyes of Galicians, constituted a part of the very same 'shield of the civilization of the West.' After the constitutional transformation of the Habsburg Empire, 1867, in the so called epoch of Galician autonomy,[29] many Galician Poles accepted such an optic. They were especially those who sympathized with the environment of the conservative daily *Czas* [*Time*] published in Cracow and the so called Cracow historical school with such historians as Walerian Kalinka, Józef Szujski, Stanisław Smolka, and Michał Bobrzyński who shaped new, critical perspectives on Polish and Galician history.[30] People who represented the aforementioned optics referred to the Enlightenment concepts of 'East' and 'West,' founding ideologically the Josephinism, but rejected the Josephinian idea of Austrians bringing civilization into the 'savage' Slavic lands. As a result, they made a shift within the East–West opposition: from their perspective, it was Galicia that was entrusted with the role of the 'bulwark' of the Western culture while Russia was attributed with the qualities of the 'East.' The latter was identified as the most dangerous enemy of Galicia. In the article from January 17, 1869 *Czas* called Russia 'the most valiant leader of brutal Asiatic force' and argued: 'Just as politically only Austria and Poland can constitute the bulwark, so economically the final outcome of the conflict

---

[28] The declaration of loyalty of the Galician Sejm on December 10, 1866 [by Adam Potocki], see *Galicja w dobie autonomicznej (1850–1914). Wybór tekstów*, ed. Stefan Kieniewicz (Wrocław: Wydawnictwo Zakładu Narodowego im. Ossolińskich, 1952), 99.

[29] See Wereszycki, *Pod berłem Habsburgów*, 179–220; Józef Buszko, "The Consequences of Galician Autonomy after 1867," *Polin* 12 (1999), 86–99.

[30] The historians of the Cracow historical school argued that the fall of the Polish-Lithuanian Commonwealth, as well as the defeat of the Polish uprising of 1830–1831 and 1863–1864 were caused by 'mistakes of the nation,' that is, anarchy and lack of respect for the state power among the nobles, see: Lawrence Wolff, "*Czas* and the Polish Perspective on the Austro-Hungarian Compromise of 1867," *Polish Review* 27, no 1–2 (1982), 65–75.

between the two currents may hang upon the strengthening of these points.'[31] This viewpoint framed the Russian thread to the region in terms of the difference between East and West and, therefore, echoed the enlightened cultural geography of the Westerners. The Polish ideal of the Polish-Lithuanian Commonwealth as *Antemurale Christianitatis* was transformed in the article into the vision of Austrian-Polish cooperation in defence of the frontiers of Western civilization. In this way *Czas* and its circles acknowledged Galicia's relationship with Austria and suggested a special, not only provincial, position of the region within the Habsburg Empire. This position was to be a base and at the same time a result of Polish culture's membership in the Western cultural circle.

After the collapse of the Habsburg Empire in 1918 and the Polish-Ukrainian war of Eastern Galicia, 1918–1919, the province was incorporated into the reborn Polish state, the Second Polish Republic. In the interwar period—in conditions of crisis of democracy, hostile policy of the Second Polish Republic towards national minorities and, in particular, antagonism between Poles and Ukrainians, and anti-Semitism—the discourse on the region (called Easter Lesser Poland[32]) was subordinate to the Polish national discourse and used to strengthen the representation of reality from the exclusive, Polish point of view.[33]

It was not until the second half of the twentieth century when the Polish intellectuals developed the discourse on Galicia, precisely speaking, the reasoning of Galician Poles of the epoch of autonomy. They started emphasizing the Western dimension of the Galician legacy in works forming the so called Galician current in the contemporary Polish literature,[34]

---

[31] *Czas*, January 17, 1869. Quoted after: Wolff, *The Idea of Galicia*, 224.
[32] Such a term was introduced to legitimate a new administrative division and underline the exclusively Polish character of the region, see: Katarzyna Hibel, *"Wojna na mapy", "wojna na słowa": Onomastyczne i międzykulturowe aspekty polityki językowej II Rzeczpospolitej w stosunku do mniejszości ukraińskiej w Galicji Wschodniej w okresie międzywojennym* (Wien, Berlin: LIT Verlag Münster, 2014), 254–256.
[33] Wierzejska, "The Idea of Galicia in the Polish Discourse, 1918–1939," the presentation at the ASA conference in Chicago, 18 March 2017.
[34] See Ewa Wiegandt, *Austria Felix, czyli o micie Galicji w polskiej prozie współczesnej* (Poznań: Wydawnictwo Naukowe UAM, 1988); Alois Woldan, *Der Österreich-Mythos in der polnischen Literatur* (Wien: Böhlau, 1996); Luiza Bialasiewicz, "Back to *Galicia Felix?*" in *Galicia: A Multicultured Land*, 160–184.

which emerged after the political 'thaw' of 1956, especially in the 1960s and 1970s.

The ideological framework of that phenomenon was constituted by the need of abreacting fundamental changes that took place in the region in the aftermath of World War II, particularly, the division of the former Galicia between the Ukrainian Soviet Socialist Republic and Communist Poland and leaving its both halves behind the Iron Curtain, in the Soviet zone of influence. In common Polish historical awareness a particular revalorization of the Habsburg Galicia made then itself felt. While in the interwar period it had been dispraised as one of the formerly annexed territories, at worse, almost deprived of martyrological tradition as opposed to Russian and Prussian part of the former Polish-Lithuanian Commonwealth, since the late 1950s it experienced unexpected appreciation. After the rise of Soviet and Nazi totalitarianisms and bloody strives of national groups in the region, the Habsburg past of the province became a byword of what Kazimierz Brandys, the Polish writer, called the 'peaceful years during the partitions era,'[35] having in mind previously Austria-, not Russia- or Prussia-occupied, territory. In comparison to the post-war scrap of the province which belonged to the Polish People's Republic, the historical Galicia, a part of the Danube Monarchy, seemed worth esteem again as an indisputable piece of the European whole and a connection between Polish and Western culture.

Initially, such ideas came to the fore in works of Polish writers who still remembered the Habsburg realities of the province. Andrzej Kuśniewicz (1904–1993), born in Eastern Galicia in a family of Polish gentry, portrayed his birthplace as a multi-national, multi-denominational *oikumene*, not only open to the West but also connected with it in many ways. For example, the protagonist of his novel *W drodze do Koryntu* [*On the way to Corinth*] (1964) is a Polish nobleman of a complex Galician identity merging provincial, imperial, and national affiliation. After World War I and II, he is aware that he belongs to a community that no longer exists. Nonetheless, he tries to recreate his formerly Galician home in

---

[35] See Kazimierz Brandys, "Spokojne lata pod zaborami," *Twórczość*, no 3 (1978), 7–40.

a different space. It is not a space, however, which is located in Eastern or even Central Europe but that which is regarded as Western: first Vienna and the Alpine borderland of Styria and Carinthia, then Verona, Paris and the French Riviera.[36]

The specifically Galician narrative developed by Kuśniewicz in his masterpieces[37] was continued by Piotr Wojciechowski (b. 1938) in his famous novel *Czaszka w czaszce* [*Skull inside a skull*] (1970), which can be classified as a kind of historiographic metafiction.[38] Wojciechowski presented Galicia at the time constituting a suggestive reconstruction of la Belle Époque. According to his vision, the province is a fully-fledged part of both the Great Empire, imaginary but very similar to the Habsburg Monarchy, though expanded to the North and the West, and the Western-oriented European mainland.[39]

Another writer, who undertook the topic of Galicia located between East and West and imbued with Western spirt, was Julian Stryjkowski (1905–1996). He was a Polish writer of Jewish origins, born in the Eastern Galician town of Stryj as a subject of Franz Joseph I. In one of his best novels, *Austeria* [*The Inn*] (1966), Austria, perceived as the ideal of 'enlightened' rule and statehood, is contrasted with the 'barbarian' regime of Russia, and Galicia is associated with the former, in sharp opposition to the latter. The protagonist of the novel, facing violence that was entailed by the encroachment of Russian ranks to the province in 1914, says indignantly: 'Here is Austria not Kishinev. And, thanks God, it will never be [Kishinev—J.W.] as long as the emperor Franz Joseph I rules here.'[40] He recalls the cruel pogrom in Kishinev in 1903, one of those organized by

---

[36] Andrzej Kuśniewicz, *W drodze do Koryntu* (Warsaw: Państwowy Instytut Wydawniczy, 1964).
[37] See also Kuśniewicz, *Strefy* (Warszawa: Państwowy Instytut Wydawniczy, 1971); Kuśniewicz, *Lekcja martwego języka* (Kraków: Wydawnictwo Literackie, 1977); Kuśniewicz, *Lesson in a Dead Language* (Venice: Marsilio Publishers, 1991); Kuśniewicz, *Mieszaniny obyczajowe* (Warszawa: Państwowy Instytut Wydawniczy, 1985).
[38] A term by Linda Hutcheon. See Linda Hutcheon, *A Poetics of Postmodernism: History, Theory, Fiction* (London, New York: Routledge, 1988).
[39] Piotr Wojciechowski, *Czaszka w czaszce* (Warsaw: Państwowy Instytut Wydawniczy, 1970).
[40] Julian Stryjkowski, *Austeria* (Warsaw: Czytelnik, 1966), 45.

the administration of the tsar Nicholas II,[41] to suggest that such atrocities are possible in Russia, that is, 'savage' East, but not in the Habsburg Empire, that is, 'civilized' West, which Galicia apparently has belonged to.

Interestingly, even though Kuśniewicz, Wojciechowski, and Stryjkowski were active in the Polish People's Republic, not in exile, their works did not arouse excessive suspicions of censorship, first and foremost, due to their formal complication. In a more conventional way the 'Western' features of Galicia were depicted, among others, in historical novels of Andrzej Stojowski[42] (1933–2006), as well as in the novel and essays of Włodzimierz Paźniewski[43] (b. 1942).

It is worth mentioning that the thread of supposed Westerness of Galicia played an important role in the debate on Central Europe, which intensified in the last two decades of the twentieth century. Milan Kundera's famous article of 1983 undermined the notion of the so called Eastern bloc and identified Central Europe, imbued with the Habsburg legacy, with a part of the West, which after 1945 was 'kidnaped' by the East.[44] Polish participants of the discussion hardly shared the opinion on immensely Western nature of Central Europe; for instance, Czesław Miłosz maintained that Western ideas getting beyond the Elba River, instead of being copied, were recast into new concepts and gained their own character.[45] Nonetheless, the Poles who engaged in the said debate did agree that the

---

[41] See: *Żydzi w Polsce Odrodzonej: działalność społeczna, gospodarcza, oświatowa i kulturalna*, vol. 2, ed. Ignacy Schiper, A. Tartakower, Aleks. Hafftka (Warszawa: „Żydzi w Polsce Odrodzonej", [1932]), 12.

[42] Andrzej Stojowski, *Podróż do Nieczajny* (Warszawa: Czytelnik, 1968); Stojowski, *Romans polski* (Warszawa: Czytelnik, 1970); Stojowski, *Chłopiec na kucu* (Warszawa: Czytelnik, 1971); Stojowski, *Kareta* (Warszawa: Czytelnik, 1972); Stojowski, *Zamek w Karpatach* (Warszawa: Czytelnik, 1973).

[43] Włodzimierz Paźniewski, *Krótkie dni* (Warszawa: Państwowy Instytut Wydawniczy, 1983).

[44] Milan Kundera, "The Tragedy of Central Europe," trans. Edmund White, *The New York Review of Books* (31) (April 26, 1984), 33–38. The article was first issued in French in 1983. See the title of the Polish translation of the text: "Zachód porwany albo tragedia Europy Środkowej," trans. M. L., *Zeszyty Literackie*, no 5 (1984), 14–31.

[45] Czesław Miłosz, "O naszej Europie," *Kultura* 463, no 4 (1986), 3–12. See also Miłosz, *Native realm: A search for self-definition*, transl. Catherine S. Leach (Berkeley: University of California Press, 1981).

heritage of the Habsburg Galicia constituted a residuum of Western values and properties in the central area of the European mainland.[46]

After the political turn of 1989, frequency of presenting Galicia as an outpost of the West in the Polish discourse decreased but it did not run out. The most important Polish author of the Galician topic nowadays, Andrzej Stasiuk, has referred to the Habsburg Galicia in many works, including *Opowieści galicyjskie* [*Tales of Galicia*] (1995),[47] the essays *O środkowej Europie* [*On Central Europe*] (2000)[48] and *Dziennik okrętowy* [*A Logbook*] (2001),[49] and the essayistic cycle *Jadąc do Babadag* [*On the Road to Babadag*] (2004).[50] In all these works, Galicia compels reflection on the central part of the continent, serving as its best synecdoche. One should keep in mind, however, that this rhetorical relationship connects neither Galicia nor Central Europe with the West. Stasiuk develops the idea of Central Europe in such a way that it could avoid the catastrophic—in his opinion—dichotomy of East versus West by linking it to the Danube River Basin and the

---

[46] For the further investigation of the debate on the Polish ground see: Aleksander Fiut, *Być (albo nie być) Środkowoeuropejczykiem* (Kraków: Wydawnictwo Literackie, 1999). Interestingly, Galicia—treated as Central Europe in a nutshell—is being entirely identified with the Western circle of values and properties by some voices in the debate which emerge in the West, see for example: 'Galicia, as Austro-Hungarian, as Western European, as not-Eastern, certainly not Russian, is thus located within the values of Western liberal thought. In contrast to the alien values of the Eastern steppes, Galicia is historical and embodied with European tradition, and "before and beyond" the Communist occupation, 1945–1991,' Luiza Bialasiewicz, John O'Loughlin, "Re-Ordering Europe's Eastern Frontier. Galician Identities and Cartographies on the Polish-Ukrainian Border," in *Boundaries and Place. European Boundaries in Geographical Context*, ed. David H. Kaplan, Jouni Häkli (London: Rowman & Littlefield Publishers, 2002), p. 221.

[47] Andrzej Stasiuk, *Opowieści galicyjskie* (Wołowiec: Czarne, 1995); Stasiuk, *Tales of Galicia*, trans. Margarita Nafpaktitis (Praha: Twisted Spoon Press, 2003).

[48] Stasiuk, "O środkowej Europie," in Stasiuk, *Tekturowy samolot* (Wołowiec: Czarne, 2002), 66–67.

[49] Stasiuk, "Dziennik okrętowy," in: Stasiuk, Yurii Andrukhovych, *Moja Europa. Dwa eseje o Europie zwanej Środkową* (Wołowiec: Czarne, 2001), 75–140.

[50] Stasiuk, *Jadąc do Babadag* (Wołowiec: Czarne, 2004); Stasiuk, *On the Road to Babadag. Travels in the Other Europe*, trans. Michael Kandel (Boston, New York: Houghton Mifflin Harcourt, 2011).

southern orientation.[51] Regardless of Stasiuk's attitude towards the issue, iterations of Western-oriented vision of the province have been still present in the young Polish literature, for example, in Łukasz Saturczak's (b. 1986) novel *Galicyjskość* [*Galicianess*] (2010). The coda of the novel, which refers to the Orange Revolution in Ukraine (2004), suggests that Galicia—although its existence is only phantomatic, confined to mentality of few inhabitants of the Polish-Ukrainian borderland—can adequately embody Europe, both Central and the one extending from London eastward to Kiev, as it represents the same European values of freedom and democracy. Therefore, a couple of Poles, who decide to support the protesters, can go against the grain of the well-established geography, along a symbolic route of the metropolises belonging to the former Habsburg Monarchy—from Przemyśl via Lviv, Cracow, Budapest, Vienna and Prague to Kiev, because 'everything is penetrated by Galicia.'[52]

Figure 12: Charles I, the last Emperor of Austria and the last King of Hungary, in Chernivtsi (1917). Public Domain.

Let us add that the similar—to some extent—image of Galicia is presented in albums, guides, and other publications mixing historical and literary

---

[51] For the further investigation of the issue see: J. Wierzejska, "Mit Południa jako kontrapunkt dla opozycji Wschód – Zachód i podstawa mitu Europy Środkowej," *Porównania* 11 (2012), 71–86.
[52] Łukasz Saturczak, *Galicyjskość* (Warszawa: Lampa i Iskra Boża, 2010), 165.

discourse in popular rather than artistic way, which have been issued many times in Poland after 1989.[53] Stressing Polish character of the province, they hint at connections between Poles and Austrians in various fields, from cultural to political, as well as at general influence Vienna and, consequently, Western Europe had on the region. What is striking, they somehow simultaneously exoticize Galicia. In order to attract readers' attention, the publications in question embellish the image of the province with references to singularity of its wild nature, thrilling oddity of the local life, and adventures waiting there for visitors. These hints refer to, first and foremost, the Eastern part of the former Galicia, especially that known as the Eastern Carpathian Mountains. It is perhaps the best confirmation that contemporary Polish discourse on the region is still deeply entangled into the old antinomy of East and West.[54]

In parallel with these phenomena in Poland, the concept of the province's European nature started to arouse interest in Western Ukraine, particularly the former Eastern Galicia that became a part of independent Ukraine, after 1991. Since the late 1980s, the concept in question has been undertaken by intellectuals of young generations creating artistic circles of the Stanislaviv Phenomenon and the Galician autonomists.[55] They appreciated borderland, peripheral location of the Habsburg Galicia, that 'ever-transitional (from hands to hands, from camp to camp) strip,'[56] at least for

---

[53] Cf. for example Grodziski, *Wzdłuż Wisły, Dniestru i Zbrucza. Wędrówki po Galicji dyliżansem, koleją* (Kraków: Wydawnictwo Bohdan Grell i Córka, 1998); Mieczysław Czuma, Leszek Mazan, *Austriackie gadanie, czyli encyklopedia galicyjska* (Kraków: Anabasis, 1998); Zbigniew Fras, *Galicja* (Wrocław: Wydawnictwo Dolnośląskie, 2003).

[54] See Jagoda Wierzejska, "'Idealized land of harmony and happiness'? Remarks on the Polish discourse on Galicia," in *Galician polyphony. Places and voices*, ed. Alina Molisak, Jagoda Wierzejska (Warszawa: Dom Wydawniczy Elipsa, 2015), 323–343.

[55] See: Ola Hnatiuk, *Pożegnanie z imperium. Ukraińskie dyskusje o tożsamości* (Lublin: Wydawnictwo Uniwersytetu Marii Curie-Skłodowskiej, 2003); Lidia Stefanowska, "Back to the Golden Age: The Discourse of Nostalgia in the 1990s" in *Contemporary Ukraine on the Cultural Map Europe*, ed. Larrisa M. L. Zaleska Onyshkevych, Maria G. Rewakowicz (New York, London: M. E. Sharpe, 2009), 119–130; Olena Fedyuk, "Stanislav Phenomenon. More on Ukrainian National Identity," *Kakanien Revisited* 25, no. 8 (2006) <http://www.kakanien.ac.at/beitr/fallstudie/OFedyuk1.pdf> (accessed October 10, 2017).

[56] Andrukhovych, Volodymyr Yeshkiliev, *Potyah 76*, no 1 (2002), 14.

two reasons. First, because—as a result of its borderland position—Galicia was determined by cultural heritage of many cohabiting national-religious groups. Second, because its marginality modelled a specific 'viewpoint form the periphery,' characterized by looking up towards the centre, on the one hand, and on the other, by assuming distanced perspective by the spectator. According to Olena Fedyuk, it was precisely the peripheral status of Galicia, entailing geographical proximity to 'the other' territorial, cultural and linguistic space, which allowed the artists of the Stanislav Phenomenon, as well as the Galician autonomists, to associate the province with the idea of Central Europe.[57] Such a move gave rise to recreating a common Central European cultural space that was assumed to exist when Galicia had belonged to the Danube Monarchy, and that Western Ukraine was a part of, due to its Galician past. Such an expanded idea of Central Europe, including Ukraine (at least the Western one), was a starting point for writing the latter back into European context, a process in which a vision of Galicia as a share of the Habsburg, undeniably European legacy had a bridging function. That historical tradition constitutes an alternative for artists who want to associate themselves neither with the Soviet system and the Russian imperialist perception of Ukrainians as 'brotherly Russian people,' nor with the homogenized nationalistic discourse that has been reinforced in Western Ukraine after 1991. According to many of these artists, the idea of Galicia's 'Westerness' paves the way to an attempt to legitimize the special status of the region and to build a kind of Galician-Western Ukrainian identity. From that perspective, the former Galicia is the only pro-western, pro-democratic, and market-oriented region of Ukraine; the one ready and eager to be accepted into the European Union in sharp contrast to Eastern pro-Russian Ukraine.[58]

---

[57] Fedyuk, "Stanislav Phenomenon. More on Ukrainian National Identity," 5.
[58] For the further discussion on the impact of Galician project on the integration process and search for a new national identity in Ukraine see Mykola Riabchuk, *Vid Malorosii do Ukrainy. Paradoksy zapizniloho natsiietvoriennia* (Kyiv: Krytyka, 2000); Mykola Riabchuk, *Dvi Ukrainy: realni mezhi virtualni igry* (Kyiv: Krytyka, 2003); Yaroslav Hrytsak, "Historical Memory and Regional Identity among Galicia's Ukrainians," in *Galicia: A Multicilturred Land*, 185–209.

The most important projects aiming at Ukraine's movement into the cultural and ideological space of Central Europe, in particular, and Europe, in general, were the Lviv journal *Ï* [*Ji*] and the periodical *Potyah 76* [*The train 76*] referring to the name of the train number 76 that run from Chernivtsi westwards to Przemyśl. Both of them, the former initiated in 1995, the latter in 2002, became the major forum dedicated to the Central European debate in the country, which outstanding artists of the Stanislav Phenomenon and the Galician autonomists participated in.

In 2002, in the special issue of *Ï* entitled *Federatyvna Respublika Ukraïna*, Taras Vozniak, the editor of the journal, opened a discussion on regional autonomy.[59] The discussion revealed that implementation of the idea of *sborna Ukraïna*[60] during the course of the previous ten years have not met the expectations of a considerably group of the Western Ukrainian intelligentsia. The contributors of the issue responded to that disappointment by searching for a separate, distinct pattern of Western Ukrainianess rooted in different temporal and geographic dimension, most often in the Habsburg period of the region's history. They expressed the opinion that from the time of the medieval Principality of Galicia-Volhynia, Western part of today's Ukraine was part and parcel of European culture and civilization, which found its most vocal testimony in the epoch when the territory was under the rule of Vienna.

A striking manifestation of that 'invented tradition'[61] of the region is delivered by Volodymyr Kostyrko (b. 1967), perhaps the most outspoken Galician autonomist. Kostyrko fosters the view that 'Galicia has belonged to the Latin, occidental civilization since the time it was Christianized'[62] and, to express it, he writes in Ukrainian using Latin alphabet instead of

---

[59] Taras Vozniak, [foreword to] *Ï. Niezalezhnyi kulturolohichnyi chasopys*, no 2 (2002): "Federatyvna Respublika Ukraïna," 4.

[60] That is, Ukraine as a union of previously tsarist, Habsburg, and other—'occupied,' according to national Ukrainian discourse—territories.

[61] See Eric Hobsbawm, "Introduction: Inventing Traditions," in *The Invention of Tradition*, ed. Eric Hobsbawm and Terence Ranger (Cambridge: Cambridge University Press, 1983), 1–14.

[62] Vlodko [Volodymyr] Kostyrko, "Ukrajinśke doktrynerstvo i Halyčyna," *Ji*, no 23 (2002), 287–288.

Cyrillic one. He argues that Galicians, due to their rootedness in the European tradition, distinctively differ from the Eastern Ukrainians and represent dissimilar, 'more intellectual' lifestyle; consequently, he concludes, they hardly fit the Ukrainian nation.[63] Kostyrko is, however, better known as a painter and a cartoonist for opinion-forming Ukrainian newspapers *Postup* [*Progress*] and *Krytyka* [*Critics*] than as a writer or journalist. His famous paintings and graphics constitute a kind of new canon of works on Galician history. One of them, titled *Złota Hałyczyna* [*Gold Galicia*] (2008), depicts the province embodied as a dignified woman in armour sitting on a throne. She holds a sword and a book in her hands, the symbols of power, freedom and wisdom, while behind her back sits a proud lion, the symbol of Lviv.[64] The picture clearly indicates ideological background of Kostyrko's art, which aim at representing an alternative Galician tradition. According to that tradition, the region marked by the Western heritage belongs to Europe and stands in a sharp contrast to the East, particularity to Russia.

Another intellectual stressing Galicia's ties to the West is Yurii Andrukhovych (b. 1960), the leader of the Stanislav Phenomenon. His volume of essays *Dezorientatsiia na mistsevosti. Sproby* [*Disorientation on Location: A Book of Essays*] (1999) provided a vision of the region as 'post-totalitarian' and 'post-multicultural' since Galicia experienced such catastrophes of the twentieth century that consigned Galician multiculturalism to the past with only its remnants and traces being left. However, due to Habsburg heritage and former diversity of the province, it remained the writer's 'last territory,'[65] that is, a base of his self-orientation and a symbol of 'better times' linking him and his favorable land with the West. Andrukhovych's nostalgia for Habsburg epoch is longing for a fortunate period of history when the city of his origins, Ivano-Frankivsk

---

[63] For further investigation of Kostyrko's views and their context see Eleonora Narvselius, *Ukrainian Intelligentsia in Post-Soviet L'viv: Narratives, Identity, and Power* (Lanham: Lexington Books, 2012), 284–285.

[64] See *Mit Galicji*, 462.

[65] Andrukhovych, *Dezorientatsiia na mistsevosti. Sproby* (Ivano-Frankivsk: Lileia-NV, 1999), 120–121.

(which he calls by its old name—Stanislaviv), 'belonged to the same state not as Tambov and Tashkent but as Venice and Vienna' and when he himself would not have needed a visa to meet Rilke or Klimt.[66] First and foremost, however, Andrukhovych's nostalgia is a need 'to look to the West,'[67] a Western Ukrainian desire—of precisely Austrian provenience[68]—to be close to, or better, to be included into the Western cultural and civilizational domain. In the later *Diiavol khovaietsia v siri. Vybrani sprobky 1999–2005 rokiv* [*The Devil is in the Cheese: Selected Essays 1999–2005*] (2007) the writer stronger, and bitterly, emphasizes Ukraine's belonging to the ex-socialist camp. Nonetheless, in his opinion, the former Galicia's links with the Habsburg Monarchy still constitute a plausible counterpoint to the model of Soviet culture, which he treats as extremely alien and superimposed. They still allows him to stay: 'we, too, are in the Atlantic zone.'[69] A suggestion of that kind, meaning that Ukrainians of Galician roots, once Austrian subjects, can today consider themselves heirs of European tradition, come to fore—albeit with distance and irony—also in his novels, for example,, *Perverziia* [*Perversion*] (1996)[70] and *Dvanadtsiat obruchiv. Roman* [*Twelve Rings. A Novel*] (2003).[71]

Apart from Andrukhovych, there were other authors coming from Western Ukraine, who undertake the concept of the Habsburg Galicia as an embodiment of Western spirit of that part of Europe. Among them Taras Prokhasko (b. 1968), Halyna Petrosanyak (b. 1969), and the daughter of the Stanislav Phenomenon's leader, Sofia Andrukhovych (b. 1982)

---

[66] Ibid., 8.
[67] Ibid.
[68] '...she [Austria—J.W.] opened new geographical possibilities for us [Ukrainians—J.W.], she taught us to look to the West with love towards its lowering twilight,' ibid.
[69] Andrukhovych, *Diiavol khovaietsia v siri. Vybrani sprobky 1999–2005 rokiv* (Kyiv: Krytyka, 2007), 208. Emphasis by the author.
[70] Andrukhovych, *Perverziia*, first edition in the journal *Suczasnist*, no 1–2 (1996); Andrukhovych, *Perverzion*, trans. Michael M. Naydan, ed. Andrew Wachtel (Evanston: Northwestern University Press, 2005).
[71] See: Andrukhovych, *Dvanadtsiat obruchiv. Roman* (Kyiv: Krytyka, 2003). For more comprehensive interpretation of the issue see Marko Pavlyshyn, "Zaklynannia Tsentralnoi Evropy: Heopolitychnyi prostir ta suchasna ukrainska literatura," in *Evropeiska melankholiia. Dyskurs ukrainskoho oktsydentalizmu*, ed. Tamara Hundorova (Stylos: Kyiv, 2008), 62–74.

are especially worth mentioning. Their books—in particular Prokhasko's novel *NeprOsti* [*The UnSimple*] (2002),[72] Petrosanyak's volume of poetry *Svitlo Okrain* [*The Light of the Outskirts*] (1998),[73] and S. Andrukhovych's novel *Feliks Avstria* [*Felix Austria*] (2014)[74]—celebrate a shared idea of Galicia, albeit interpreted individually. It is an idea of territory which, notwithstanding its geographical location, is Western, European, not Eastern, and for certain not Russian by its nature. The territory understood in such a way proves to give the aforementioned writers and their readers a sense of distance towards the former pole of the East–West opposition. It cannot, however, escape that very opposition.

Conclusions

Inscribing Galicia into the East-West opposition is as old as the Enlightenment. In the last third of the eighteenth century, presentation of the province as 'backward East' waiting for support from more developed western neighbours made Galicia into an object of civilizing mission, legitimized its conquest and integration with Austria. Therefore, it constituted a manifestation of symbolic violence against the region. The impact and effectiveness of Galicia's socio-political adaptation to the Danube Monarchy in the framework of the Josephinism is disputable. However, the ideological and cultural dimension of adaptation in question seems to be influential up until now. The contrast between 'barbaric East' and 'civilized West' has remained the conceptual framework of the province long after it ceased to exist as a geopolitical entity. For decades it has made newcomers and Galicians themselves perceive the land in terms of categories imposed on Galicia in order to align it with the imperial goals and socio-political and cultural visions of the Habsburgs. Interestingly, these categories turned out to be prone to quite divergent understanding and, over time, began to serve not only as a proof of 'Easterness' of Galicia and the necessity of the civ-

---

[72] Taras Prokhasko, *NeprOsti* (Ivano-Frankivsk: Lileia NV, 2002).
[73] Halyna Petrosanyak, *Svitlo Okrain* (Ivano-Frankivsk: Lileia NV, 2000 [1998]).
[74] Sofia Andrukhovych, *Feliks Avstria* (Lviv: Vydavnyytstvo Staroho Leva, 2014).

ilizing mission in the province, but also as an evidence of Galicia's 'Westerness' and its membership in the cultural circle of Europe. Shifting Galicia from the 'negative,' 'Eastern' pole of that opposition to the 'positive,' 'Western' one affirms the region and raises its value in the perspective of its inhabitants. On the other hand, however, it strengthens the perception of the land in terms of allegedly inescapable contradiction between East and West. As a result, even nowadays reflection on the Polish-Ukrainian borderland perpetuates such a pattern of thinking and repeats hypothesis of 'Western spirit' of this 'Eastern land' ideologically rooted in the cultural geography of the late eighteenth century.

Abstract

The article discusses the phenomenon of locating Galicia within dialectical tension between 'East' and 'West', that is, the categories of heavily ideologized cultural geography, which respectively symbolize 'backwardness' and 'development', 'barbarism' and 'civilization,' 'chaos' and 'order.' The categories in question go back to the Enlightenment. Since the creation of the province in question in 1772, Austrians justified the annexation of Polish lands by their civilizing mission, presenting Austria's rule as a remedy for alleged backwardness of that 'Eastern' land. Such a strategy for decades has made newcomers and the Galicians themselves perceive the land in terms of notions imposed upon Galicia in order to adjust the region to the imperial policies and socio-political and cultural visions of the Habsburgs. Interestingly, these notions turned out to be susceptible to divergence interpretations and, over time, began to serve not only as a proof of 'Easterness' of Galicia and the necessity of civilizing mission in the province, but also as an evidence of Galicia's 'Westerness' and its belonging to the same cultural circle as Vienna. The article delivers analysis of several examples of inscribing Galicia into the dichotomous system of meanings connected with 'East' and 'West,' from Josephinism fostered by Germanophone literature, to contemporary ideas of Polish and Ukrainian intellectuals treating Galician legacy as an entry-card to Europe.

Keywords: Galicia, imagined space, East–West distinction, travel literature, Enlightenment, backwardness, Habsburg Empire, contemporary Ukrainian literature, contemporary Polish literature

Bibliography

Amar, Tarik Cyril. *The Paradox of Ukrainian Lviv: A Borderland City between Stalinists, Nazis, and Nationalists*. New York: Cornell University Press 2015.

Andrukhovych, Yurii. *Perverziia*. First edition in the journal *Suczasnist*, no. 1–2 (1996).

Andrukhovych, Yurii. *Perverzion*. Translated by Michael M. Naydan. DeKalb: Northwestern University Press 2005.

Andrukhovych, Yurii. *Dezorientatsiia na mistsevosti. Sproby*. Ivano-Frankivsk: Lileia-NV 1999.

Andrukhovych, Yurii, Volodymyr Yeshkiliev, *Potyah 76*, no. 1 (2002).

Andrukhovych, Yurii. *Dvanadtsiat obruchiv. Roman*. Kyiv: Krytyka 2003.

Andrukhovych, Yurii. *Diiavol khovaietsia v siri. Vybrani sprobky 1999–2005 rokiv*. Kyiv: Krytyka 2007.

Andrukhovych, Sofia. *Feliks Avstria*. Lviv: Vydavnyytstvo Staroho Leva 2014.

Bialasiewicz, Luiza, John O'Loughlin, "Re-Ordering Europe's Eastern Frontier. Galician Identities and Cartographies on the Polish-Ukrainian Border." in *Boundaries and Place. European Boundaries in Geographical Context*, ed. David H. Kaplan and Jouni Häkli. London: Rowman & Littlefield Publishers 2002.

Bialasiewicz, Luiza, "Back to *Galicia Felix*?" in *Galicia: A Multicultured Land*, ed. Christopher Hann and Paul R. Magocsi. Toronto, Buffalo et al.: Toronto University Press 2005, 160–184.

Brandys, Kazimierz, "Spokojne lata pod zaborami." *Twórczość,* no 3 (1978): 7–40.

Buszko, Józef, "The Consequences of Galician Autonomy after 1867." *Polin* 12 (1999): 86–99.

Czuma, Mieczysław, Leszek Mazan. *Austriackie gadanie, czyli encyklopedia galicyjska.* Kraków: Anabasis 1998.

Fedyuk, Olena, "Stanislav Phenomenon. More on Ukrainian National Identity." *Kakanien Revisited* 25, no. 8 (2006), http://www.kakanie n.ac.at/beitr/fallstudie/OFedyuk1.pdf (acc. 10.10.2017).

Fiut, Aleksander. *Być (albo nie być) Środkowoeuropejczykiem.* Kraków: Wydawnictwo Literackie 1999.

Franzos, Karl E.. *Aus Halb-Asien. Kulturbilder aus Galizien, der Bukowina, Südrussland und Rumänien.* Leipzig: Duncker & Humblot 1876.

Franzos, Karl E.. *Vom Don zur Donau. Neue Kulturbilder aus Halb-Asien.* Leipzig: Duncker & Humblot 1878.

Franzos, Karl E.. *Aus der grossen Ebene. Neue Kulturbilder aus Halb-Asien.* Leipzig: Duncker & Humblot 1888.

Fras, Zbigniew. *Galicja.* Wrocław: Wydawnictwo Dolnośląskie 2003.

Grodziski, Stanisław. *Historia ustroju społeczno-politycznego Galicji 1772–1918.* Wrocław: Zakład Narodowy im. Ossolińskich 1971.

Grodziski, Stanisław. *Sejm Krajowy galicyjski 1861–1914.* Vol. 1. Warszawa: Wydawnictwo Sejmowe 1993.

Grodziski, Stanisław. *Wzdłuż Wisły, Dniestru i Zbrucza. Wędrówki po Galicji dyliżansem, koleją.* Kraków: Wydawnictwo Bohdan Grell I Córka 1998.

Hagen, William W. "The Moral Economy of Popular Violence: The Pogrom in Lwów, November 1918." in *Antisemitism and its Opponents in Modern Poland,* ed. Robert Blobaum. Ithaca, London: Cornell University Press 2005, 124–147.

Heffernan, Michael. *The Meaning of Europe: Geography and Geopolitics.* London: Arnold 1998.

Hibel, Katarzyna. *"Wojna na mapy", "wojna na słowa": Onomastyczne i międzykulturowe aspekty polityki językowej II Rzeczpospolitej w stosunku do mniejszości ukraińskiej w Galicji Wschodniej w okresie międzywojennym.* Wien, Berlin: LIT Verlag Münster 2014.

Hnatiuk, Ola. *Pożegnanie z imperium. Ukraińske dyskusje o tożsamości.* Lublin: Wydawnictwo Uniwersytetu Marii Curie-Skłodowskiej 2003.

Hobsbawm, Eric, "Introduction: Inventing Traditions." in *The Invention of Tradition*, ed. Eric Hobsbawm and Terence Ranger. Cambridge: Cambridge University Press 1983, 1–14.

Hrytsak, Yaroslav, "Historical Memory and Regional Identity among Galicia's Ukrainians." in *Galicia: A Multicultured Land*, ed. Christopher Hann and Paul R. Magocsi. Toronto, Buffalo et al.: Toronto University Press 2005, 185–209.

Hubert, Stanisław. *Poglądy na prawo narodów w Polsce czasów Oświecenia.* Wrocław: Zakład Narodowy im. Ossolińskich 1960.

Hutcheon, Linda. *A Poetics of Postmodernism: History, Theory, Fiction.* London, New York: Routledge 1988.

Kieniewicz, Stefan, ed. *Galicja w dobie autonomicznej (1850–1914). Wybór tekstów*. Wrocław: Wydawnictwo Zakładu Narodowego im. Ossolińskich 1952.

Kłańska, Maria. *Daleko od Wiednia. Galicja w oczach pisarzy niemieckojęzycznych 1772–1918*. Kraków: Universitas 1991.

Kłańska, Maria, "Die deutschsprachige Literatur Galiziens und der Bukowina von 1772 bis 1945." in *Deutsche Geschichte im Osten Europas. Galizien, Bukowina, Moldau*, ed. Isabel Röskau-Rydel. Berlin: Siedler Verlag 1999, 381–482.

Kostyrko, Vlodko [Volodymyr], "Ukrajinśke doktrynerstvo i Halyčyna." *Ji*, no. 23 (2002): 287–288.

Kozłowski, Maciej. *Między Sanem a Zbruczem. Walki o Lwów i Galicję Wschodnią 1918–1919*. Kraków: Znak 1990.

Kratter, Franz, *Briefe über den itzigen Zustand von Galizien*. Leipzig: Verlag G. Ph. Wucherers 1786; Reprint: Berlin: Helmut Scherer Publishing House 1990.

Kundera, Milan, "The Tragedy of Central Europe." Translated by Edmund White. *New York Review of Books* 31/7 (April 26, 1984): 3–38.

Kundera, Milan, "Zachód porwany albo tragedia Europy Środkowej," Translated by M. L., *Zeszyty Literackie*, no 5 (1984): 14–31.

Kuśniewicz, Andrzej. *W drodze do Koryntu*. Warszawa: Państwowy Instytut Wydawniczy 1964.

Kuśniewicz, Andrzej. *Strefy*. Warszawa: Państwowy Instytut Wydawniczy 1971.

Kuśniewicz, Andrzej. *Lekcja martwego języka*. Kraków: Wydawnictwo Literackie 1977.

Kuśniewicz, Andrzej. *Mieszaniny obyczajowe*. Warszawa: Państwowy Instytut Wydawniczy 1985.

Kuśniewicz, Andrzej. *Lesson in a Dead Language*. Venice: Marsilio Publishers 1991.

Paźniewski, Włodzimierz. *Krótkie dni*. Warszawa: Państwowy Instytut Wydawniczy 1983.

Pavlyshyn, Marko, "Zaklynannia Tsentralnoi Evropy: Heopolitychnyi prostir ta suchasna ukrainska literature." in *Evropeiska melankholiia. Dyskurs ukrainskoho oktsydentalizmu*, ed. Tamara Hundorova. Stylos: Kyiv 2008, 62–74.

Petrosanyak, Halyna. *Svitlo Okrain*. Ivano-Frankivsk: Lileia NV, 2000 [1998].

Prokhasko, Taras. *NeprOsti*. Ivano-Frankivsk: Lileia NV 2002.

Prusin, Alexander V.. *Nationalizing a Borderland: War, Ethnicity, and Anti-Jewish Violence in East Galicia, 1914–1920*. Tuscaloosa: University of Alabama Press 2005, 75–91.

Riabchuk, Mykola. *Vid Malorosii do Ukrainy. Paradoksy zapizniloho natsiietvoriennia*. Kyiv: Krytyka 2000.

Riabchuk, Mykola. *Dvi Ukrainy: realni mezhi virtualni igry*. Kyiv: Krytyka 2003.

Magocsi, Paul R.. *Galicia: A Historical Survey and Bibliographical Guide*. Toronto, Buffalo et al.: University of Toronto Press 1983.

Magocsi, Paul R.. *A History of Ukraine*. Toronto, Buffalo et al.: University of Toronto Press 1996.

Magocsi, Paul R., "Galicia: A European Land." in *Galicia: A Multicultured Land*, ed. Christopher Hann and Paul R. Magocsi. Toronto, Buffalo et al.: Toronto University Press 2005, 7–9.

Maner, Hans-Christian, "Włączenie Galicji do monarchii habsburskiej w XVIII wieku." in *Mit Galicji*, ed. Jacek Purchla, Wolfgang Kos et al. Kraków: Międzynarodowe Centrum Kultury 2014, 139–144.

Mick, Christoph. *Lemberg, Lwów, L'viv, 1914–1947: Violence and Ethnicity in a Contested City*. West Lafayette: Purdue University Press 2016.

Miłosz, Czesław. *Native realm: A search for self-definition*, Translated by Catherine S. Leach Berkeley: University of California Press 1981.

Miłosz, Czesław, "O naszej Europie." *Kultura* 463, no. 4 (1986): 3–12.

Narvselius, Eleonora. *Ukrainian Intelligentsia in Post-Soviet L'viv: Narratives, Identity, and Power*. Lanham: Lexington Books 2012.

Said, Edward. *Orientalism: Western Concepts of the Orient*. New York: Pantheon Books 1978.

Saturczak, Łukasz. *Galicyjskość*. Warszawa: Lampa i Iskra Boża 2010.

Schiper, Ignacy, A. Tartakower et al., ed. *Żydzi w Polsce Odrodzonej: działalność społeczna, gospodarcza, oświatowa i kulturalna*. Vol. 2. Warszawa: „Żydzi w Polsce Odrodzonej" [1932].

Schnür-Pepłowski, Stanisław. *Galiciana 1778–1812*. Lviv: H. Altenberg 1897.

Schnür-Pepłowski, Stanisław. *Cudzoziemcy w Galicyi 1787–1841*. Kraków: Spółka Wydawnicza Polska 1902

Stasiuk, Andrzej. *Opowieści galicyjskie*. Wołowiec: Czarne 1995.

Stasiuk, Andrzej. *Tales of Galicia*. Translated by Margarita Nafpaktitis. Praha: Twisted Spoon Press 2003.

Stasiuk, Andrzej, "Dziennik okrętowy." in *Moja Europa. Dwa eseje o Europie zwanej Środkową*, Jurij Andruchowycz and Andrzej Stasiuk, Wołowiec: Czarne 2001, 75–140.

Stasiuk, Andrzej, "O środkowej Europie." in *Tekturowy samolot*, Andrzej Stasiuk. Wołowiec: Czarne 2002, 66–67.

Stasiuk, Andrzej. *Jadąc do Babadag*. Wołowiec: Czarne 2004.

Stasiuk, Andrzej. *On the Road to Babadag. Travels in the Other Europe*. Translated by Michael Kandel. Boston, New York: Houghton Mifflin Harcourt 2011.

Steiner, Carl. *Karl Emil Franzos, 1848–1904: Emancipator and Assimilationist*. New York: Peter Lang 1990.

Stefanowska, Lidia, "Back to the Golden Age: The Discourse of Nostalgia in the 1990s." in *Contemporary Ukraine on the Cultural Map Europe*, ed. Larrisa M. L. Zaleska Onyshkevych and Maria G. Rewakowicz. New York, London: M. E. Sharpe 2009, 119–130.

Stojowski, Andrzej. *Podróż do Nieczajny*. Warszawa: Czytelnik 1968.

Stojowski, Andrzej. *Romans polski*. Warszawa: Czytelnik 1970.

Stojowski, Andrzej. *Chłopiec na kucu*. Warszawa: Czytelnik 1971.

Stojowski, Andrzej. *Kareta*. Warszawa: Czytelnik 1972.

Stojowski, Andrzej. *Zamek w Karpatach*. Warszawa: Czytelnik 1973.

Stryjkowski Julian. *Austeria*. Warszawa: Czytelnik 1966.

Traunpaur, Alphons H. *Dreyssig Briefe über Galizien: oder Beobachtungen eines unpartheyischen Mannes, der sich mehr als nur ein paar Monate in diesem Königreiche umgesehen hat*. Wien, Leipzig: G. Wucherer und E. Beer 1787; Reprint: Berlin: Helmut Scherer Publishing House 1990.

Vozniak, Taras, "Foreword." *Ї. Niezalezhnyi kulturolohichnyi chasopys*, no. 2 (2002): "Federatyvna Respublika Ukraïna."

Vushko, Iryna. *The Politics of Cultural Retreat: Imperial Bureaucracy in Austrian Galicia 1772–1867*. New Haven, London: Yale University Press 2015.

Wereszycki, Henryk. *Pod berłem Habsburgów. Zagadnienia narodowościowe*. Kraków: Wysoki Zamek 2015, 33–46.

Wiegandt, Ewa. *Austria Felix, czyli o micie Galicji w polskiej prozie współczesnej*. Poznań: Wydawnictwo Naukowe Uniwersytetu Adama Mickiewicza 1988.

Wierzejska, Jagoda, "Mit południa jako kontrapunkt dla opozycji Wschód-Zachód i podstawa mitu Europy Środkowej." *Porównania 11* (2012): 71–86.

Wierzejska, Jagoda, "'Idealized land of harmony and happiness'? Remarks on the Polish discourse on Galicia." in *Galician polyphony. Places and voices*, ed. Alina Molisak and Jagoda Wierzejska. Warszawa: Dom Wydawniczy Elipsa 2015, 323–343.

Wierzejska, Jagoda, "Walki polsko-ukraińskie o Lwów w literaturze dla dzieci i młodzieży dwudziestolecia międzywojennego." *Bibliotekarz Podlaski* 33, no. 2 (2016): 97–118.

Wierzejska, Jagoda, "The Idea of Galicia in the Polish Discourse, 1918–1939." Presentation at the ASA conference in Chicago, 18 March 2017.

Wojciechowski, Piotr. *Czaszka w czaszce.* Warszawa: Państwowy Instytut Wydawniczy 1970.

Woldan, Alois. *Der Österreich-Mythos in der polnischen Literatur.* Wien: Böhlau 1996.

Wolff, Lawrence, "*Czas* and the Polish Perspective on the Austro-Hungarian Compromise of 1867." *Polish Review* 27, no. 1–2 (1982): 65–75.

Wolff, Larry. *Inventing Eastern Europe: The Map of Civilization on the Mind of the Enlightenment.* Stanford: Stanford University Press 1994.

Wolff, Larry, "Inventing Galicia: Messianic Josephinism and the Recasting of Partitioned Poland." *Slavic Review* 63, no. 4 (2004): 818–840.

Wolff, Larry. *The Idea of Galicia: History and Fantasy in Habsburg Political Culture.* Stanford: Stanford University Press 2010.

Zayarnyuk, Andriy, "Imperium, chłopi, ruchy narodowe – galicyjski trójkąt postkolonialny?" *Historyka* 42 (2012): 101–113.

Magdalena Baran-Szołtys
University of Vienna, Austria

ANDRZEJ STASIUK'S GALICIAN 'MIDDLE EUROPE': HALF-DARK, EMPTY, AND BOUNDLESS

Introduction

> If I had to invent an emblem for Middle Europe, I would put in the one-half darkness and in the other emptiness. The first one as a sign of non-obviousness, the second as one for an until now, untamed space. A beautiful emblem with slightly fainted contours which one can fill with his own imagination. Or with his dreams.[1]

This statement from the essay *Dziennik okrętowy*[2] [*Log Book*] (2000) by Andrzej Stasiuk (b. 1960) describes his vision of 'Middle Europe:' a microcosm, which enables an imaginative, historical-philosophical re-construction of 'Other Europe.' It is intended to be read in the context of Europe's 1989 political reconfiguration. This period inspired a noteworthy shift in literary interest in geography; which led to literature starting to construct geographical spaces, in which the concept of Central Europe is prominent. In this article I will focus on three questions, which will stake new ground in the existing body of work on Stasiuk, but also build on and update existing conclusions:

(1) What does East and West mean in this context and what meanings do those ideas have in Stasiuk's poetics?
(2) What are the main features of Stasiuk's Middle Europe and why did he choose these features?
(3 How is Stasiuk's Middle Europe connected to the pre-existing concepts of Austrian Galicia, Kresy, and Sarmatia, and how does it differentiate itself from the popular concept of Central Europe?

---

[1] Andrzej Stasiuk, „Dziennik okrętowy," in *Moja Europa. Dwa eseje o Europie zwanej Środkową*, Jurij Andruchowycz and Andrzej Stasiuk (Wołowiec: Czarne, 2000), 102. (Unless otherwise noted all translations from Polish and German in this article are my own—M.B.-S.)
[2] Ibid.

I will argue that Stasiuk's 'Middle European' space is (as quoted above) defined by 'non-obviousness' and an 'untamed space' 'with slightly fainted contours.' On the one side, this 'untamed space' is connected to the mythologizing concepts of Austrian Galicia or the Habsburg Empire in general as well as his Middle European 'nowhere.' On the other, the 'Middle European' space is limited by restrictive concepts of East and West, and oscillating between these two definitive concepts.

Figure 13: *Mohort* (1859) by January Suchodolski (1797–1875). Public Domain.

I will draw mainly on Stasiuk's works from the 1990s because I will later argue that these works represent a different space and a different kind of Central Europe compared to his later publications. My analysis will focus on three of his works: the programmatic essay *Dziennik okrętowy*, in which he attempts to conceptualise his own poetics, as well as the stories *Dukla*

(1997)[3] and *Opowieści galicyjskie*[4] [*Tales of Galicia*[5]] (1996). I will use the term 'Middle Europe' when referring to Stasiuk's concept and 'Central Europe' for general references to the topographical region or the concept defined anew in the 1980s and re-discovered by Milan Kundera.[6]

Magdalena Marszałek points out that after the years 1989 / 1991, there is a process of self-discovery in Central Europe—the part of the continent inspired by the changes of the political landscape. Thus Stasiuk's essays paradigmatically represent the new literary mapping of Eastern Europe.[7] Therefore, my analysis focuses solely on Stasiuk's work from the 1990s as a negotiation of Polishness after the transition of 1989. The historical region of old Austrian Galicia plays an important but not exclusive role in this negotiation. In the 1990s and in the early 2000s, Stasiuk focused on the Beskid Mountains and the post-Galician space. Therefore, his concept of 'Middle Europe' from that time is based on these two regions. However, beginning with *Jadąc do Babadag*[8] (2004) Stasiuk's travel narratives start to reach further south,[9] incorporating south-eastern Europe into the constructed 'Middle Europe' and as Jagoda Wierzejska argues,[10] this provides an alternative to the linear East-West dichotomy. His latest publications deal with regions further east: *Wschód*[11] [*East*] (2014) relates to Russia, China, and Mongolia, *Osiołkiem*[12] [*On a Donkey*] (2016) covers Russia, Ukraine, and Asia.

---

[3] Andrzej Stasiuk, *Dukla* (Gładyszów: Czarne, 1997).
[4] Andrzej Stasiuk, *Opowieści galicyjskie* (Kraków: Znak, 1995).
[5] Andrzej Stasiuk, *Tales of Galicia*, trans. by Margarita Nafpaktitis (Prague: Twisted Spoon Press, 2003).
[6] Milan Kundera, "The Tragedy of Central Europe," *New York Review of Books* 31/7 (April 26, 1984): 3–38. First published in French with the title "Un Occident kidnappé ou la tragédie de l'Europe centrale," in *Le Débat* 27 (1983).
[7] Magdalena Marszałek, "Anderes Europa. Zur (ost)mitteleuropäischen Geopoetik," in *Geopoetiken. Geographische Entwürfe in den mittel- und osteuropäischen Literaturen*, ed. Magdalena Marszałek and Sylvia Sasse (Berlin: Kadmos, 2010), 45.
[8] Andrzej Stasiuk, *Jadąc do Babadag* (Wołowiec: Czarne, 2004).
[9] See: Stasiuk, *Jadąc do Babadag*; Andrzej Stasiuk, *Fado* (Wołowiec: Czarne, 2006); Andrzej Stasiuk, *Dziennik pisany później* (Wołowiec: Czarne, 2010).
[10] See: Jagoda Wierzejska, "Mit południa jako kontrapunkt dla opozycji Wschód-Zachód i podstawa mitu Europy Środkowej," *Porównania 11* (2012): 71–86.
[11] Andrzej Stasiuk, *Wschód* (Wołowiec: Czarne, 2014).
[12] Andrzej Stasiuk, *Osiołkem* (Wołowiec: Czarne, 2016).

Galicia, Kresy, Sarmatia

Stasiuk's self-defined and self-proclaimed 'Middle Europe' intermingles with traditions of myth producing, transnational constructs like Sarmatia and Kresy. Although these constructs are often used to define a similar idea, they are referring to different concepts.

Galicia refers to the crownland Galicia and Lodomeria (1772–1918) which was an administrative region of the Habsburg Empire. Although this superficial and constructed character was derived from this region from the very beginning, as Larry Wolff prominently stated,[13] today Galicia features an after-life in many national narratives and hence is a transnational phenomenon. Texts about travels to Austrian Galicia have been published since the late eighteenth century and influenced the representation of Galicia, both within and beyond the province. After 1989 a new wave of publications arose that explored Galicia; but even these contemporary texts and travels focus on a historical space that no longer exists. Nevertheless, this (post-)Galician space remains popular for travelers and 100 years later the Habsburg heritage still plays a crucial role during these travels and within the texts. Travelers are constantly updating the pre-established images and ensuring the continued existence of Galicia, with its specific Habsburg features. The old travel accounts used to present Galicia as the periphery of Austria-Hungary. The province was characterized as 'wild,' 'backward' and 'barbaric.'[14] These publications suggested that Galicia was a distinctive Eastern territory that needed to be enlightened and civilized by the new rulers. The contemporary travel narratives have been slowly transforming this picture. Galicia has become a nostalgic place, similar to Atlantis: a world of memory of one's childhood, literature and

---

[13] Larry Wolff, "Inventing Galicia. Messianic Josephinism and the Recasting of Partitioned Poland," *Slavic Review* 63/3 (2004): 818–840; Larry Wolff, *The Idea of Galicia. History and Fantasy in Habsburg Political Culture* (Stanford: Stanford University Press, 2010).

[14] Elisabeth Haid, Stephanie Weismann et al., "Einleitung," in *Galizien. Peripherie der Moderne – Moderne der Peripherie?*, ed. Elisabeth Haid, Stephanie Weismann et al. (Marburg: Herder, 2013), 1.

history.[15] Andrzej Stasiuk's texts are part of this broader phenomenon. Multiethnicity and multilingualism are topics closely connected to the imperial Austria-Hungary in these new travelogues, being one of the Empire's main features in these spatial narratives from the late twentieth century. In this multiethnicity, Jewish people have played a preeminent role. The Habsburg times are depicted as an opposition to the traumatic events following the collapse of the Empire. Stasiuk invokes the Habsburg heritage of the Danube Monarchy (so called 'Kakania'), especially the old Austrian crownland Galicia and Lodomeria as a basis for his literary construction of Europe outside the East-West dichotomy. Anti-historical, idiosyncratic descriptions based on personal memory dominate his perception of Galicia. The transnational (post-)Galicia is meant to be an integral part of 'Middle Europe.' Stasiuk locates his 'Middle Europe' exactly in the 'historical ephemeral Galicia, which becomes an manifestation of the historical and geographical unstable Middle Europe.'[16]

---

[15] Alois Woldan, "Nachwort," in *Europa erlesen. Galizien*, ed. Stefan Simonek and Alois Woldan (Klagenfurt: Wieser, 1998), 203; Krzysztof Lipiński, "Die 'Habsburgische Atlantis' in Galizien," in *Galizien als gemeinsame Literaturlandschaft*, ed. Fridrun Rinner and Klaus Zerinschek (Innsbruck: Institut für Sprachwissenschaft der Universität Innsbruck, 1988), 55–64.

[16] Marszałek, "Anderes Europa," 56

Figure 14: Lemkos, an East Slavic minority of the Carpathian Mountains. Public Domain.

Galicia and the Kresy[17] are two interrelated historiographical and mystifying concepts that often overlap in contemporary public discourse. They are clearly separated in their development, but both played an important role in the formation of Polish national identity. As memory spaces, they take on important functions in the national narrative by belonging to the Polish myth of the East,[18] while Galicia is often seen as part of the Kresy in Polish

---

[17] The term Kresy refers to the former Polish eastern territories, which are referred to in Polish as 'Kresy (Wschodnie)' or simply as 'kresy'. The 'kresy' of the Polish–Lithuanian Commonwealth taken up by Wincenty Pol are to be distinguished in their historical meaning. See: Christof Schimsheimer, "Galicia and the Kresy as Polish places of memory in comparison," in *Galizien in Bewegung. Wahrnehmungen – Begegnungen – Verflechtungen*, ed. Magdalena Baran-Szołtys, Olena Dvoretska et al. (Göttingen: Vienna University Press at V&R unipress, 2018), 37–55.

[18] Ibid.

discourse.[19] While Galicia goes back to the actual existing crown land of Galicia and Lodomeria, the Kresy was originally founded on a legend about the knight Mohort. Between 1840 and 1852, Wincenty Pol wrote the poem *Rapsod rycerski z podania*[20] (1854), which transformed this legend into literature and described how Mohort defended the southeastern borders of the Polish-Lithuanian Commonwealth. This poem spread relatively quickly in the second half of the nineteenth century, became very popular and is influencing the afterlife of the Kresy until today.[21] Still this concept remains problematic for Ukraine, Belarus, and Lithuania, because it determines a relation which may be read as symbolic of Polish colonialism. The term Kresy is in itself politically incorrect and shows a solely Polish perspective.[22]

The myth of Galicia, in contrast to that of the Kresy, came into use only after 1918 and after 1945–1948 as well as after 1989 even stronger.[23] In the Polish People's Republic, Galicia and the Kresy were not widely used in public discourse. Kresy were almost completely marginalized until the 1980s. The memory thus existed within the private sphere or found its way into intellectual circles, where these concepts stood for freedom and the historical Polish glories. The theme grew in popularity after the fall of the Iron Curtain 1989 / 1991, which was reflected in a wide range of publications such as picture books, travel guides, travelogues and memoirs, but

---

[19] Janusz Golec, *Od Wiednia do Czerniowiec. Galicja i Bukowina w wybranych niemieckojęzycznych utworach literackich* (Lublin: UMCS, 2017), 7–8.
[20] Wincenty Pol, *Mohort. Rapsod rycerski z podania* (Warszawa: M. Arct, 1909).
[21] Jacek Kolbuszewski, *Kresy* (Wrocław: Wydawnictwo Dolnośląskie, 1995), 6.
[22] Bogusław Bakuła, "Colonial and Postcolonial Aspects of Polish Borderland Stodies: An Outline," in *Teksty Drugie* 1 (2014): 96–123.
[23] See: Grzegorz Kowal, "Mit(y) Galicji," in *Pogranicza, Kresy, Wschód a idee Europy*, ed. Anna Janicka, Grzegorz Kowalski et al. (Białystok: Książnica Podlaska im. Łukasza Górnickiego, 2013), 609–652; Jacek Purchla, "Ein Galizien nach Galizien. Über den einzigartigen Mythos von einem 'verschwundenen Königreich,'" in *Mythos Galizien*, ed. Jacek Purchla, Wolfgang Kos et al. (Wien, Kraków: Wien Museum, 2015), 49–53; Elżbieta Wiącek and Karolina Golemo, "Galicja for ever—nostalgiczny sen o utraconej Arkadii, moda na monarchię czy atrakcja turystyczna?" in *Semiotyczna mapa Małopolski*, ed. Elżbieta Wiącek (Kraków: Ksiegarnia Akademicka, 2015), 141–223; Adam Kożuchowski and Werner Nell, "Galizien. Zerrissene und wiedergefundene Geschichten," in *Deutsch-Polnische Erinnerungsorte. Geteilt/Gemeinsam*, ed. Hans Henning Hahn and Robert Traba (Paderborn: Ferdinand Schöningh, 2015), 177–196.

also in numerous reprints of old works. However, the territory covered in these publications also includes that of Galicia and thus also affects this part of Polish history.[24] Academia has focused predominantly on this topic in relation to the relationship between the Kresy and the newly populated formerly German eastern territories,[25] as well as its postcolonial significance.[26]

The spatial positioning of both concepts, Galicia and Kresy, seems problematic, since both, as is often the case with memory spaces, go beyond physical territory boundaries. It is clear, however, that the eastern part of Galicia, now part of the Ukraine, is a part of the Kresy, which means that during the journeys in the post-Galician area these two memory spaces are interwoven in the travelogues. The Kresy are always build on a poetic basis, from which they descend, as Jacek Kolbuszewski points out: 'Meaning space, kresy are often a metaphor, more frequently even an ambiguous symbol. So it seems that the word kresy even in its ordinary usage preserved the status of the element of the poetic language.'[27] But the territorial boundary position contained in the term is only one of its many characteristics in Polish:[28] 'It is noteworthy that the expression of the

---

[24] This is particularly evident in publications dedicated to the Galician territory or cities such as Lwów or Stanisławów. See: Sławomir Koper, *Spacer po Lwowie. Przewodnik po Kresach* (Warszawa: Axel Springer, 2008).

[25] See: Jarosław Syrnyk, *Ludność ukraińska na Dolnym Śląsku (1945–1989)* (Wrocław: IPN, 2007); *Vertreibungen aus dem Osten Deutsche und Polen erinnern sich*, ed. Hans-Jürgen Bömelburg, Renate Stößinger et al. (Olsztyn: Borussia, 2000); Ewa Nowicka and Aleksandra Bilewicz, *Pamięć utraconych ojczyzn* (Warszawa: WUW, 2012); Włodzimierz Suleja, "Trudny proces zakorzenienia. Kresowiacy na Dolnym Śląsku," in *Kresowe dziedzictwo. Studia nad językiem, historią i kulturą*, ed. Anna Burzyńska-Kamienicka, Małgorzata Misiak et al. (Wrocław: ATUT, 2012), 269–275.

[26°] See: Bogusław Bakuła, "Colonial and Postcolonial Aspectsof Polish Discourse on the 'Borderlands,'" in *From Sovietology to Postcoloniality. Poland and Ukraine from a Postcolonial Perspective*, ed. Janusz Korek (Stockholm: Södertörn hogskóla 2007), 41–59; Grażyna Borkowska, "Perspektywa postkolonialna na gruncie polskim – pytania sceptyka," *Teksty Drugie* 5 (2010): 40–52; Dorota Kołodziejczyk, "Postkolonialny transfer na Europę Środkowo-Wschodnią," *Teksty Drugie* 5 (2010): 22–39; Hanna Gosk, "Postcolonial or Postdependency Studies," *Teksty Drugie* 1 (2014): 235–247.

[27] Jacek Kolbuszewski, "Kresy– pojęcie, znaczenia, wartości," in *Kresowe dziedzictwo. Studia nad językiem, historią i kulturą*, ed. Anna Burzyńska-Kamienicka and Małgorzata Misiak (Wrocław: ATUT, 2012), 13.

[28] On the genesis of the term and its change of meaning see: Kolbuszewski, *Kresy*; Kolbuszewski, *Kresy – pojęcie, znaczenia, wartości*; Stefan Kieniewicz, "Kresy.

meaning of the Polish Borderlands does not include the foreign word equivalents of the word (e.g. eng. *Borderland*, ger. *Grenzland*, fr. *confin*, sk. *pohraničie*, lv. *pierobežas apgabali* etc.).'[29] This is only the confirmation of their function as a memory space similar to their Galician equivalent.

Figure 15: Former Greek Catholic Church in Wołowiec. Licensed under CC BY 3.0.

The Polish myth of the East is evident not only in the culture of Kresy or even Galicia (if perceived within its peripheral discourse), but also in Polishness itself which is characterized, as Maria Janion describes: a 'Western Easternness or Eastern Westernness…The notion of the divid-

---

'Przemiany terminologiczne w perspektywie dziejowej," *Przegląd Wschodni* 1 (1991), 3–13; Marek Wedemann, "Gdzie leży Beresteczko? Kresy na mapie," in *Kresy. Dekonstrukcja*, ed. Krzysztof Trybuś, Jerzy Kałążny et al. (Poznań: Poznańskie Towarzystwo Przyjaciół Nauk Redakcja Wydawnictw, 2007), 11–35.

[29] Kolbuszewski, *Kresy– pojęcie, znaczenia, wartości*, 13.

ing border blurs into a borderland. It means transculturation, the penetration of cultures, hybridity and an equivocation of this creation.'[30] Returning to Stasiuk, his 'Middle Europe' includes all of these features. Stasiuk stated in an interview in 2015: 'Poland is constituted by the East and the West, but in my opinion more by the East.'[31] Eventually, this is the perspective Stasiuk leans towards in the last years of his publications while in the 1990s he combines both East and West in his configuration of other Europe.

'In the ironical-nostalgic invocation of the Middle European otherness one can hear the old voice of Sarmatia,'[32] states Marszałek creating thereby a new construct with this appearance. As Dirk Uffelmann outlines, Sarmatism was a 'cultural formation'[33] which was 'encompassing ideological self-definition, political life, and everyday culture among Polish nobleman from the mid-sixteenth century until the third partition at the end of the eighteenth century.'[34] First it was seen as part of a wider phenomenon influencing the nobility of many other contemporary states like Moldavia, Hungary, or Wallachia, later it was constructed as a feature typical of Polish culture. Today, Sarmatism is a mythogene, poetic name for premodern Poland and is linked to the nobility of the Polish–Lithuanian Commonwealth. Sarmatism is also closely connected to Polish self-orientalization and thus to Orientalism. From the seventeenth century onwards, Poles practiced self-orientalization but at the same time were subjected to an Easternization by the Westerners. Poles travelling to Western Europe in the seventeenth and eighteenth century were perceived as Turks.[35] Sabine Jagodzinski explains this phenomenon which is combined with her own

---

[30] Maria Janion, "Sarmaci na pograniczu," in *Niesamowita Słowiańszczyzna. Fantazmaty literatury,* Maria Janion (Kraków: Wydawnictwo Literackie, 2007), 177.
[31] Agnieszka Cytacka, "Nie wiadomo, po co się jedzie. Z Andrzejem Stasiukiem rozmawia Agnieszka Cytacka," in *Czytanie Literatury* 4 (2015): 244.
[32] Marszałek, "Anderes Europa," 67.
[33] Janusz Maciejewski, "Sarmatyzm jako formacja kulturowa," *Teksty* 4 (1974): 19. Translated into English by Dirk Uffelmann.
[34] Dirk Uffelmann, "'Here you have all my stuff!'. Real Things from a Mythical Country: Ottoman 'Sarmatica' in Enlightened Poland," in *Präsenz und Evidenz fremder Dinge im Europa des 18. Jahrhunderts, ed.* Birgit Neumann (Göttingen: Wallstein, 2015), 325.
[35] Ibid., 323–25.

fascination with the Orient and their self-orientalization which was visible in their exterior appearance (such as clothing).[36] Even this diachrononical view exposes Polish's (self)positioning between East and West as something that evolved through history. Jakub Niedźwiedź goes one step further: he examines Sarmatism as a 'invented (national) tradition.' From this perspective, Sarmatism is a narrative about Poland and Poland's past invented by the nineteenth and twentieth century.[37] This perspective unites Sarmatism with Larry Wolff's version of Galicia and Wincenty Pol's legend of Mohort and the Kresy. Stasiuk's Middle Europe echoes many of these notions.

The concepts around these 'mythogene, transnational constructs' of Sarmatia, Kresy, and Galicia are interrelated. Though the term *Kresy* is disputable, Galicia can be transnationally conceptualised without evoking any controversies.[38] So it is the Kakanian past whose intrinsic feature is its transnationalism: 'The visibility of the Kakanian heritage should not mainly generate […] imperial nostalgia or culturally hegemonic impulses, but more inspire the thinking in transnational categories.'[39] When referring to these concepts in connection with Stasiuk, his own self-definition or the definition of his own Europe becomes visible, as well as his strategies of construction and mythologizing which are inherent to Galicia, Kresy and Sarmatia. In his poetics, these imaginary spaces offer different kinds of possibilities for constructing not only his own past and identity, but also different futures, and at the same time being a *terra incognita* with its 'non-obviousness' 'untamed space' and 'slightly fainted contours,' to use Stasiuk's word from the opening quote.

---

[36] Sabine Jagodzinski, "Mit den Waffen des Gegners – Orientalische Elemente und Gedenken der Türkenkriege in der polnischen Adelskultur des 17. Jhs.," in *Sarmatismus versus Orientalismus in Mitteleuropa / Sarmatyzm versus Orientalizm w Europie Środkowej*, ed. Magdalena Długosz and Piotr O. Scholz with the assistance of Martin Faber (Berlin: Frank & Timme, 2012), 318.

[37] Jakub Niedźwiedź, "Sarmatyzm, czyli tradycja wynaleziona," *Teksty Drugie* 1 (2015): 46–62.

[38] Marszałek, "Anderes Europa," 56.

[39] Roman Dubasevych, "Über Erinnerung in die Postmoderne. Paradigmen der westukrainischen Literatur nach der Wende," in *Galizien. Fragmente eines diskursiven Raums*, ed. Doktoratskolleg Galizien (Innsbruck et al.: Studien Verlag, 2009), 220.

Stasiuk's Geopoetics: Now vs. Then

'And how could they, just like this, decide not to let me back home again? Because I am at home here—it is not their Europe, but my Europe, our Europe, a different Europe. And it is good that she exists', writes Yurii Andrukhovych (b. 1960) in his essay *Z nienapisanej książki Granice Europy* [*From the Unwritten Book Borders of Europe*].[40] At the beginning of the twentieth first century Andrzej Stasiuk and Yurii Andrukhovych declared that 'the so called Middle Europe' lies between the East and the West. *Moja Europa. Dwa eseje o Europie zwanej Środkową* [*My Europe. Two essays about the so called Middle Europe*][41] was the name of their 'literary double portrait' written by the Polish Galician author and his Ukrainian counterpart, published for the first time in the year 2000. The use of the term 'so called' in the title, suggests a demarcating approach to the term 'Middle' or 'Central;' 'my' refers the private and individual character of this Europe.[42] In these two essays, both authors attempt to characterise 'their' own (post-)Galician space and what they call 'their Europe.' This is their attempt to position their ideas and poetics within the discourse of Middle- and Central Europe. Fifteen years after the first publication of the essay, Stasiuk does not feel the same way about it: 'Sometimes I kick myself that Yurii Andrukhovych and I have written *My Europe*. Because of that book we have been pigeonholed as Middle European writers,'[43] he stated in 2015. Indeed, until today both writers are linked to Galicia and Central Europe in the public's mind, although the emphasis and focus of their works has since changed, especially in Stasiuk's case.

Today, Stasiuk is considered a mediator between the East and the West. As a publisher and writer, he influences the perception of both, East and West, in Poland and beyond. In fact, he presents the 'other Europe' and

---

[40] Jurij Andruchowycz, "Z nienapisanej książki Granice Europy," in *Diabeł tkwi w serze*, Jurij Andruchowycz, (Wołowiec: Czarne, 2007), 21.
[41] Andruchowycz and Stasiuk, *Moja Europa*.
[42] In this paper I am using the term 'Middle Europe' when referring to Stasiuk's concept of this part of Europe, as it is a literal translation of the Polish term *Europa Środkowa*.
[43] Andrzej Stasiuk and Dorota Wodecka, *Życie to jednak strata jest* (Wołowiec: Czarne, 2015), 148.

the East to the West. In 2016, Andrzej Stasiuk received the Austrian State Prize for European Literature awarded by the Federal Chancellery for Arts, Culture, and Media to European writers. For the first time since 1988 (28 years on) it was again awarded to a Polish writer. The prize was established in 1965 in a Cold War dominated Europe: 'Therewith we hoped to get once again into conversation with our neighbours from behind the Iron Curtain,' Thomas Drozda, Austrian Ministry of Culture, stated during the award ceremony in Salzburg in July 2016.[44] The political significance of the prize cannot be questioned. Hence it does not seem coincidental that in times of the 'refugee crisis' and the rise of the right wing nationalism, particularly but not only in the so-called Visegrád Group, it was awarded to one of the most internationally acclaimed contemporary Polish writers. Additionally to one who is best known for his travels to territories which in the West are usually understood as Eastern Europe. The concept of Eastern Europe is dominated by the former borders of the socialist block and includes Central and Southern Europe as well as Russia. The reason for awarding it to Stasiuk was described by the minister himself: 'The works of Andrzej Stasiuk have essentially contributed to the eastward enlargement of our literary perception of the world.' To put it simply, it seems that Andrzej Stasiuk demonstrates to the 'West' what the 'East' looks like. His literary travels through the 'Wild East' of Europe gain the function of old travelogues from the Enlightenment sharing pictures of the 'rediscovered' *terra incognita*. At the same time, Stasiuk seems to be instrumentalized for the 'eastward enlargement' of the West since he writes about European unity with a unique Central Europe as part of it. 'While it may be seductive for author and reader alike,' his way of writing and acting 'tacitly reproduces stereotypes that have been present in the discourse prevalent in Western Europe since the Enlightenment,'[45] states Jagoda Wierzejska in one of her

---

[44] It is worth mentioning that this prize went more frequently to Polish writers. In 1965 the first prize went to Zbigniew Herbert; more Poles followed: Sławomir Mrożek (1972), Tadeusz Różewicz (1982), Stanisław Lem (1985) and Andrzej Szczypiorski (1988).

[45] Jagoda Wierzejska, "(Post-)bordering Galicia in Ukrainian and Polish post-colonial discourse: The cases of Yurii Andrukhovych and Andrzej Stasiuk," *Journal of European Studies* 47/2 (2017):182.

analyses about Stasiuk's relationship with concepts of Europeanisms. As a publisher Andrzej Stasiuk (together with his wife, the anthropologist Monika Sznajdermann) runs a publishing house Czarne[46] and also attempts to popularize Central and Eastern European literature in Poland. From the outset, the publishing house has concentrated on publications from young and also already highly esteemed authors from Central, Eastern and Southern Europe: Yurii Andrukhovych, Svetlana Alexievich, Ivan Čolov, Irena Karpa, Danilo Kiš, Jáchym Topol, Taras Prochasko, Natalka Sniadanko, Dubravka Ugrešič, Aglaja Veteranyi, Serhiy Zhadan, for example. The series *Inna Europa. Inna Literatura* [*Other Europe. Other Literature*] is the publishing house's trademark with a characteristic logo: a horse-drawn vehicle with a peasant as an ironic symbol of backwardness.[47] The popularity and impact of Czarne in the Polish literature landscape revealed itself during the nominations to the Nike Award, the most important Polish literature award, in 2016. Out of 20 nominated titles, six were from the publishing house Czarne; from the titles that eventually received awards, two were from Czarne.[48]

It is clear that Stasiuk's work has influenced the perception of Central and Eastern Europe in Western Europe, implying a political dimension of his work: geopoetics always stands in a relationship to geopolitics. In the context of Stasiuk's work, Magdalena Marszałek applied the term 'geopoetics,' arguing that one has to turn the politics into poetics or to make the poetics 'do' the politics.[49] Stasiuk's 'Middle European poetic' is meant to be positioned between the 'capitalist, liberal West' and the 'Post-Soviet, spiritual East,' which highlights a connection in the post-socialistic realities. This connection is between the previously dominating spirituality / materialism and the now dominating commercialization / liberalism. This

---

[46] The name *Czarne* goes back to the name of a former Lemko village in the Lower Beskids, not far away from where Stasiuk lives now in Wołowiec and where the publishing house is stationed.

[47] See: Czarne, http://czarne.com.pl/ (April 9, 2016); Gerhard Gnauck, "Der Ruf der Beskiden," *Neue Zürcher Zeitung*, August 16 (2012), www.nzz.ch/feuilleton/buecher/der-ruf-der-beskiden-1.17482029 (April 9, 2016).

[48] Nike Nagroda Literacka, "Nike 2016," http://www.nike.org.pl/strona.php?p=29&eid=23 (February 21, 2017).

[49] Marszałek, "Anderes Europa," 66.

division highlights the founder of geopoetics Kenneth White himself summarizing the goals of the ideology of progress for both as follows:

> In Marxist Russia, it would be the creation of a great State whose mission would be to put an end to all States and usher in World Communism. In the liberal West, it would be some kind of immense Supermarket, offering a package deal of happiness to all (providing you kept in line and didn't criticize the management).[50]

Today, only one of these ideologies remains: 'The Marxist light faded into greater and greater gloom in the latter years of the twentieth century, and then suddenly sputtered out. Only the Supermarket still stands on the horizon.'[51] The narrators in Stasiuk's texts enter the ambivalent worlds that Kenneth White describes: they have already left one world, but have not really yet entered the other which creates the space in-between, the emptiness and unboundless, to use the comparisons from *Dziennik okrętowy*. Further, Stasiuk's narrators could be classified as 'intellectual nomads,' a term introduced by Kenneth White:

> These figures are difficult to define and impossible to classify. They are not professional, without being vaguely amateurish. They are not persons, they are subjects. [...] The nomadic subject is an intention and a trajectory [...,] a field of energy.[52]

This nomadic subject concentrates on fundamental questions and the world, trying to think outside of dichotomies and finding new solutions for today's world culture:

> What could be the central motif, the central concern for a world-culture today, able to be shared by all, North, South, East and West? A reasonable answer, an obvious answer one might say, would be: the very Earth on which we try to live. Hence the *geo* in geopoetics.[53]

Stasiuk's texts concentrate on the 'geo,' as they focus on concrete space, and on the people living in poverty at the 'imagined' peripheries of Europe who are often torn between past and present, new and old order. However,

---

[50] Kenneth White, "An Outline of Geopoetics," in *The International Institute of Geopoetics*, http://institut-geopoetique.org/en/articles-en/37-an-outline-of-geopoetics (November 10, 2017), n.p.
[51] Ibid.
[52] Ibid.
[53] Ibid.

Stasiuk often digresses from this subject to elaborate more on the Habsburgian history of this space and on private memories from his own childhood and youth. These elements construct his idiosyncratic 'Middle Europe:' the attempt to overcome the East / West opposition as well as the reliance on the cultural, collective heritage of Galicia, Kresy and Sarmatia by connecting both through the concept of his private geography with imaginary flashbacks from his personal memories.

Further, we may keep in mind the centre and periphery opposition which was theorized extensively by the Russian theorist of geopoetics Igor' Sid. He concludes that the periphery is the productive ground for creativity,[54] which fits with Stasiuk's works as well as his private life. Edward Said's 'imaginary geography' also plays a meaningful role since the periphery is often the subject of orientalisation,[55] even more when it is based on geohistorical and geocultural constructs like Europe, Sarmatia or Orient.[56] Although Stasiuk's texts are geopoetical and not geocultural,[57] depending on categories like Europe or Galicia his work relates to a geopolitical dimension.[58]

---

[54] Igor' Sid and the group Poluostrov, "Osnovnoy vopros geopoetiki," in *Pervay a konferentsiya po geopoetike* (Moskva, Krymskiy klub, April 24.04.1996), http://liter.net/geopoetics/penin.html (February 21, 2017), n.p.
[55] Edward Said, *Orientalism* (SNew York: Pantheon Books, 1978).
[56] Susi K. Frank, "Geokulturologie – Geopoetik. Definitions- und Abgrenzungsvorschläge," in *Geopoetiken. Geographische Entwürfe in den mittel- und osteuropäischen Literaturen*, ed. Magdalena Marszałek and Sylvia Sasse (Berlin: Kadmos, 2010), 34.
[57] See: Magdalena Marszałek, "'Pamięć, meteorologia oraz urojenia': środkowoeuropejska geopoetyka Andrzeja Stasiuka," in *Literatura, kultura i język polski w kontekstach i kontaktach światowych*, ed. Małgorzata Czermińska, Katarzyna Meller et al. (Poznań: Wydawnictwo Naukowe UAM 2007), 539–547; Marszałek, "Anderes Europa," 43–67; Magdalena Marszałek, "Der Schriftsteller als Geograph und Gastarbeiter: Die literarische Kartographie Andrzej Stasiuks," in *Germanoslavica. Zeitschrift für germano-slavische Studien* 21/1–2 (2010): 146–156.
[58] See: Oksana Weretiuk, "Jurij Andruchowycz i Andrzej Stasiuk o tożsamości ukształtowanej przez historię," *Porównania* 9 (2011): 89–100; Christof Schimsheimer, "Die Galizische Geschichte: zur Reproduktion literarischer und historischer Narrative am Beispiel von Andrzej Stasiuks Prosa," in *Galizien als Kultur- und Gedächtnislandschaft im kultur- und sprachwissenschaftlichen Diskurs*, ed. Ruth Büttner and Anna Hanus, (Frankfurt am Main: Peter Lang 2015), 261–281.

For his 'Middle Europe' from the 1990s, this means an oscillation not only between East and West but also centre and periphery, past and present. Alfrun Kliems describes Stasiuk's literary works from the 1990s as characterized by 'anti-urbanism, underground aesthetic, and regional determinism' which tend to 'produce structural aggressive fantasies of a reruralized 'East'[59] This anti-urbanism leads to a focus on the periphery which is present in all of Stasiuk's texts, not only the ones from the 1990s.

'My own middle Europe' vs. the East, the West, and Central Europe

In his works from the 1990s Stasiuk's 'Middle Europe' was largely identical to the (post-)Galician space, and takes advantage of the Habsburg heritage in these regions. The reference to Austria-Hungary is one of his methods to position himself and his imagined Europe outside the East-West opposition.

Stasiuk's 'Middle Europe' is private: to find the center of it, he sticks a compass in the place where he lives (Wołowiec), and extends it to where he was born (Warsaw), everything in this circle is his *Europa Środkowa*, his 'Middle Europe:'

> So I pick the needle in the place where I am now, and everything indicates that I will remain. I place the second arm where I was born and where I have spent most of my life. This is finally the basic size when we try to reconcile our own biography with space. A distance of about three hundred kilometers is in straight line lays between my Wołowiec and Warsaw. Obviously, I cannot resist the temptation, so I plot a three hundred-kilometer circle around Wołowiec to determine my own Middle Europe.[60]

In this circle you have towns such as Cluj-Napoca, Arad, Szeged, Budapest, Žilina, Katowice, but you do not find Germany or Russia.[61] In the perhaps most quoted passage of his essay *Dziennik okrętowy*, the features

---

[59] Alfrun Kliems, "Aggressiver Lokalismus: Undergroundästhetik, Antiurbanismus und Regionsbehauptung bei Andrzej Stasiuk und Jurij Andruchovyč," *Zeitschrift für Slawistik* 56/2 (2011): 197.
[60] Stasiuk, "Dziennik okrętowy," 77–78.
[61] Ibid.

of Stasiuk's 'Middle Europe' become evident: it is 'private' and a 'space in-between,'[62] between the East and the West, which seems quite obvious. It is distinctive that he calls it 'swoją środkową Europę,' so 'my own middle Europe,' in distinction to the term 'Europa Środkowa' ('Middle Europe'), although he uses also this term many times during his essay.[63] Therefore in his definition he puts the emphasis on 'my own' which suggests the strong personal connection to the space and the individual definition of this space. 'Middle Europe' suggest also the personal relationship to space which comes from inside of one person: 'we try to pair our own biography with space.'[64] This demonstrates Stasiuk's concept of his Europe: it definitely lies outside the given concepts of Central Europe, East, and West, although he himself mentions them.

Further in the essay, the narrator describes the East as a space 'intertwined by a boundlessness,' in which 'everything seems the same.' In contrast, the West is 'a little bit different, but not obligatorily better.' He does not see the point of travelling there, because in the East one is 'defeated by space' and in the West 'overpowered by time.' It is a space where 'everything was already discovered two or three times.'[65] So the only space one can travel to is the space in-between: his 'Middle Europe' in contrast is a space open for discoveries, somehow a *tabula rasa* that can include everything one wants to put in it, especially his own past. Stasiuk's poetics always focus on three major themes: time, space and memory, and as the result his 'Middle Europe' is dominated by these topics. By connecting them Stasiuk invokes the Habsburg heritage. It is an attempt to return to the times before the split of East and West, before Middle Europe became 'an outpost of the socialist and capitalist camp,'[66] as the historian Karl Schlögel puts it. Stasiuk's concept of Middle Europe differs from Kundera's concept of Central Europe that positions Central Europe politically

---

[62] Marszałek, "Anderes Europa," 52.
[63] E.g. Stasiuk, "Dziennik okrętowy," 101, 111, 131.
[64] Ibid., 77.
[65] Ibid. 85.
[66] Karl Schlögel, "Lehrstück I. Fall der Berliner Mauer 1989," in *Im Raume lesen wir die Zeit*, Karl Schlögel (München: Hanser, 2003), 25.

in the East but culturally in the West.[67] Stasiuk's 'Middle Europe' is intellectually not oriented towards the West: 'To be a Middle European means: to live between the East which never existed and the West which existed for too long.'[68] The concept tries to distance oneself from all these fixed ideas and construct a new type of Europe. Nevertheless Stasiuk's work always stays political. His European concept needs the East and the West opposition to define itself. Wierzejska encapsulates this condition for Stasiuk and Andruchovyč: 'Both writers cannot therefore free themselves from thinking in terms of the East-West opposition, which shows their postcolonial attitude, indicating that they require a binary world-image for the purposes of politics, ideology, and mythology.'[69]

Galicia as part of the Habsburg Monarchy is an alternative to the East-West dichotomy and works for both authors as a basis of their construction of a Europe outside this dichotomy. It resembles a 'ship, which is exposed to flows and winds East-West and back,' but constitutes a center that 'actually is the one and only real land.'[70] The 'real' seems to be the most important part here, because this is the only thing one can truly rely on, and demonstrates land and people, in contrast to the abstract concepts of East, West and Central Europe. Jagoda Wierzejska captures also this point: 'Stasiuk's skepticism regarding European unity leads to an image of Central European uniqueness.'[71]

Therefore, different political-historical and cultural concepts assigned to this space are mixed up. Stasiuk uses the term *Europa Środkowa*, 'Middle Europe', and positions himself inside the discourse, at the same time strengthening his polemical position: 'Middle Europe was no way the same as my Central Europe, because it was only an envoy of the hyperreal West,'[72] he writes in *Dziennik okrętowy* and shows his awareness of the

---

[67] Kundera, "The Tragedy of Central Europe," 3–38.
[68] Stasiuk, "Dziennik okrętowy," 136.
[69] Jagoda Wierzejska, "Central European Palimpsests: Postcolonial Discourse in Works by Andrzej Stasiuk and Yurii Andrukhovych," in *Postcolonial Europe? Essays on Post-Communism Literatures and Cultures*, ed. Dobrota Pucherová and Róbert Gáfrik (Leiden, Boston: Koninklijke Brill, 2015), 385.
[70] Ibid.
[71] Wierzejska, "(Post-)bordering Galicia," 183.
[72] Stasiuk, "Dziennik okrętowy," 135–136.

debate. Through the twentieth century the term *Mitteleuropa* has a long history in German-speaking Europe,[73] and was never able to lose the lingering association of hegemonic and conquest politics.[74] Although Stasiuk uses 'my Central Europe' in this sentence, in contrast to 'Middle Europe' as influenced by the 'West', in the essay he uses 'Middle Europe' to refer to his concept of this space. By switching this terms their randomness is uncovered.

In *Moje Europa* Andruchovyč und Stasiuk are further constructing a 'literary Middle Europe,' quoting the publishing house Suhrkamp.[75] 'We drove 60 kilometers an hour through a world constructed to pitch the needs of a text,' Stasiuk states in *Dziennik okrętowy* and reveals one more time the geopolitical character of the text. This Middle European world is a borderland similar to the undefinable Kresy, but is much bigger than that. Michał Olszewski puts it straight: 'for Stasiuk boundlessness is a state of mind [...]. It is an aversion against the center, an escape to cultural and geographical peripheries.'[76] Also Wierzejska points out the same feature: 'The verdict of the Otherness of 'their' Europe in turn leads the authors to verify the ideal fluidity and flexibility of boundaries.'[77] This boundlessness is also visible in Stasiuk's travels and works which are ever-expanding over time. In the 1990s they started in Wołowiec and covered primarily the Lower Besikds[78], today they are reaching as far as China.[79]

---

[73] See: Joseph Partsch, *Mitteleuropa. Die Länder und Völker von den Westalpen und dem Balkan bis an den Kanal und das Kurische Haff* (Ghota: Perthes, 1904); Friedrich Naumann, *Mitteleuropa* (Berlin: Reimer, 1915).
[74] Karl Schlögel, "Karten monochrom: der Nationalstaat," in *Im Raume lesen wir die Zeit*, 199–210, 206.
[75] Juri Andruchowytsch and Andrzej Stasiuk, *Mein Europa. Zwei Essays über das sogenannte Mitteleuropa*. (Frankfurt am Main: Suhrkamp, 2004), cover text.
[76] Michał Olszewski, "Eseje o równowadze (Jurij Andruchowycz, Andrzej Stasiuk – 'Moja Europa')," *Studium* 5–6 (2000): 130–131.
[77] Wierzejska, "(Post-)bordering Galicia," 186.
[78] See: Andrzej Stasiuk, *Biały kruk* (Poznań: Biblioteka Czasu Kultury, 1995); Stasiuk, *Opowieści galicyjskie*; Andrzej Stasiuk, *Przez rzekę* (Gładyszów: Czarne, 1996); Stasiuk, *Dukla*; Stasiuk, "Dziennik okrętowy,"; Andrzej Stasiuk, *Tekturowy Samolot*. (Wołowiec: Czarne, 2000); Andrzej Stasiuk: *Zima i inne opowiadania* (Wołowiec: Czarne, 2001).
[79] See: Stasiuk's *Wschód* and *Osiołkiem*.

Stasiuk's Middle Europe is geographically undefined and limited, it is an intellectual phenomenon based on space but not limited to a certain extent of space. This space is expanding but covers always similar features: domination of periphery and borderless, a chronotopic character of space ('geography fights with history,'[80]) the denouement of West and East into an idiosyncratic 'Middle Europe,' prevalent decay and the focus on the Kakanian heritage. It transforms into a microcosm being the basis for his imaginative, historical-philosophical deliberations. Therefore, he is using cultural memory and individual memories from his own biography, inscribing 'Middle Europe' in his texts through melancholy, nostalgia and poetics based on ruins.

Figure 16: Tomb effigy of Amalia Mniszech (1736–1772) in Saint Mary Magdalene Church in Dukla. Made by Jan Obrocki in 1773. Licensed under CC BY 3.0.

---

[80] Olszewski, "Eseje o równowadze," 133.

Stasiuk's Collective Galicia: a Creative Construction of Cultural Past

Stasiuk uses the domination of Habsburg Empire over other powers in Central Europe, to fill it with his own stories: Stasiuk's post-Galician space is empty and boundless, so it can be filled with whatever one wants. Stasiuk fills it on the one hand with personal memories, on the other with concepts of his 'Middle Europe' or references to the times of the Habsburg past that are usually connected to trans-nationalism and the Jewish heritage, as well as the historical Austrian Galicia with its multiethnicity and Emperor.

In *Dziennik okrętowy* the narrator recalls the Empire a couple of times. For example as looking at the weather forecast in television and concluding: 'It rains almost in the whole Empire.'[81] Later of he tries to 'reimagine a summer day one hundred years ago:'[82]

> I am standing at the window of the town's inn and watching as the wagon drivers on the muddy common land harness horses and cover the cargoes on the wagon with tarpaulins. They tell Hungarian, perhaps also Slovak, Hungarian or Polish words to themselves. [...] It is the eighteenth of August: the birthday of his majesty.[83]

The text reconstructs this passed world in a narrative way but reflects on it from today's perspective: 'The countries of the Habsburgs are slowly swelling like diseased arteries and trying to lead their own lives. Article XIX of the Constitution is like a timed bomb, and this bomb will tear the monarchy to pieces.'[84] It is a creative construction of public, cultural past of this space in the text. The author presents an imagined world of the past, often by quoting other texts, like the following example shows:

> You drink a beer at the Graniczna, walk out onto the market square, and your imagination swells like a balloon in a physics lesson, [...]: One-horse dorozhka from Iwonicz 3 crowns, two-horse dorozhka 7 crowns, stagecoach one crown fifty. The stagecoach departs at 6:00 a.m., 7:30 a.m., and 2:00 p.m. One may spend the night at Lichtmann's inn for one crown fifty, and eat in Henryk the Musician's breakfast

---

[81] Stasiuk, "Dziennik okrętowy," 122.
[82] Ibid.
[83] Ibid, 122–123.
[84] Ibid., 126–127.

room. Three thousand inhabitants, of whom two and a half thousand are Jews. The year is, let's say, 1910.[85]

Stasiuk is constructing this world, in a very mnemonic manner, as still during the Habsburg Empire, even though the text is based almost one to one on an old travel guide for Galicia by Mieczysław Orłowicz from the year 1919: 'The One-horse dorozhka from Iwonicz to Dukla costs 3 K, two-horse 7 K, in the stagecoach 1.50 K; They depart from Iwonicz 6 and 7:30 am and 2 pm. Inn Lichtmanna with a restaurant (room 1.50 -2 K), further a restaurant in the Casino and room for breakfast at Henryk Muzyk's.'[86] It seems that the historical references in Stasiuk's *Dukla* are mainly based on Orłowicz's description of the town Dukla in his travel-guide.[87] Dukla with its Jewish community from around 1910 is poetically revived. This Jewish heritage is also represented through Kamil Targosz's illustrations in the book. Dukla itself is a small town, which hundred years ago was part of the Habsburg Empire and Western Galicia. Back then more than half of the population was Jewish.[88] During World War II the town was almost completely destroyed: in 1950 only 560 people lived there.[89] Today it has around 2.000 inhabitants and the Jewish heritage is almost not visible,[90] but recalled in the text.

However, the narrator points out that this re-reference does not particularly interest him in relation to the place: 'When I keep revisiting Dukla, then, I don't care about the stagecoaches, or the Jews, or any of that. I'm only interested in whether time is a disposable item [...].'[91] Using the text

---

[85] Stasiuk, *Dukla*, 52.
[86] Mieczysław Orłowicz, *Ilustrowany przewodnik po Galicji, Bukowinie, Spiszu, Orawie i Śląsku Cieszyńskim* (Lviv: Akademicki Klub Turystyczny w Lwowie, 1919), 380–384, 380.
[87] He might have also used: Emmanuel Swieykowski, *Monografia Dukli, Studya do historyi sztuki i kultury wieku osiemnastego w Polsce* (Kraków: Akademia umiejętności, 1903).
[88] In 1990, 2.600 out of 3.300 inhabitants were Jews. See: Orłowicz, *Ilustrowany przewodnik po Galicji*, 380.
[89] "Miejscowości Gminy Dukla," Serwis informacyjny Gminy Dukla, http://www.dukla.pl/gmina_okolice.php?no=4 (acc. 09.11.2017).
[90] "Dane statystyczne," Serwis informacyjny Gminy Dukla, http://www.dukla.pl/gmina_okolice.php?no=5 (acc. 09.11.2017).
[91] Stasiuk, *Dukla*, 53.

as a playground he is also transforming collective memories connected with his own memory among them. This way of his acquisitions of space can be well observed at the figure of Amalia Brühl and her sarcophagus[92] in *Dukla,* where she plays a key role for the nostalgic narrator and for the text. They are used as a link between the past and the present but are more than that: 'Memory links the personal and the public,'[93] Dennis Walder argues. That means that Amalia's imagined resurrection in the text simultaneously symbolizes an individual appropriation of space as well as a creative transformation of historical heritage and personal memories. The sarcophagus of Amalia encodes the memory and makes the remembrance come alive. The function of details like this is revealed in the text itself through the imagined resurrection of Amalia:

> […] and I saw Amelia sit up on her bed. [...] She stretched. Her cap fell off and her long hair spilled onto her shoulders. […] her magnetic skeleton attracted elementary particles out of the surrounding space and reassembled her body of old. […]. Everything I had seen in life, everything others had seen, was entering into her and assuming shape. […] A resurrection has to consist of something. [...] All the dead, all things that have passed forever, […] everything that once was and will never be again, was now being transformed into her body.[94]

Aside from this imagined metaphor of the revived personal and collective memory—though not only memory, but the past in general, even things not remembered and not stored—the narrator describes his perception of Amalia: 'Amalia was not a ghost or a phantom. She was the condensed

---

[92] Amalia Brühl refers to the intriguing historical figure of Maria Amalia Mniszchowa (1736–1772), who was the wife of *mareschalus curiae* Jerzy August Mniszech, a politically highly influential figure and the owner of Dukla. The Mniszech Family moved to Dukla after the death of Augustus III and was from that moment on responsible for the town's flourishing development. Through their engagement and their investments (the rebuilding of the city, the building of the palace as well as art purchases) the small town became the center of the region. See: Maria Czaplińska, "Mniszchowa z Brühlów Maria Amelia," in *Polski Słownik Biograficzny,* Vol. 21, ed. Emanuel Rostworski (Wrocław et al.: PAN/PAU, 1976), 454; Jerzy Kowalczyk, "Die Bedeutung des wettinischen Königshofes für den kulturellen und künstlerischen Austausch – Polen in Sachsen, Sachsen in Polen," in *Die Personalunionen von Sachsen-Polen 1697–1763 und Hannover-England 1714–1837. Ein Vergleich,* ed. Rex Rexheuser (Wiesbaden: Harrassowitz, 2005), 217.

[93] Dennis Walder, "Remembering Rousseau. Nostalgia and the Responsibilities of the Self," *Third World Quarterly* 26/3 (2005): 423.

[94] Stasiuk, *Dukla,* 103.

presence of that which was always absent. She was a picture that was moving back toward its model so as to exceed it.'[95] What the narrator exemplifies could be a definition of nostalgia—a longing for something that in this form might have never existed, but is reimagined in an idealized state, also in a metaphysical kind of way. Svetlana Boym calls it reflective nostalgia.[96] A 'meditation on history and the passage of time'[97] in the perception of the narrator is the essential feature of *Dukla* specifically and of Stasiuk's oeuvre in general, which here is epitomized in the figure of Amalia, her sarcophagus and her resurrection.[98] Additionally, they symbolize an individual appropriation of space and a creative play with historical places and people:

> Dukla was ceasing to exist beyond the wall. It had entered into her [Amalia] along with all the other events I'd lived through; I've watched as they moved away one by one to their tranquil annihilation. And at no point did I ever think of a way to revive them, none except memory–that bastard of time over which no one ever has any power.[99]

The memory carries the story and is so closely linked to space and time that it unites both. Further, the sarcophagus is the most evident reification of memory but in the context of Stasiuk's text *Dukla* as a whole represents reification. 'Because it was all like a living grave, like something put to sleep forever,'[100] the narrator states while recalling his first love in a public shower where he and his beloved once met. He makes it even more obvious in the following passage: 'Dukla is filled with space in which images

---

[95] Ibid.
[96] Svetlana Boym, *The Future of Nostalgia* (New York: Basic Books, 2001), 49.
[97] Ibid.
[98] For an extended analysis of nostalgia in Stasiuk's Dukla see: Magdalena Baran-Szołtys, "Visions of the Past: Revised in the Present, Recreated for the Future. Nostalgia for and Travels to Galicia in Polish Literature after 1989," in *Galizien in Bewegung. Wahrnehmungen – Begegnungen – Verflechtungen*, ed. Magdalena Baran-Szołtys, Olena Dvoretska et al. (Göttingen: Vienna University Press at V&R unipress, 2018), 75–90. For nostalgia in Stasiuk's works in general: Lidia Stefanowska, "Back to the Golden Age: the Discourse of Nostalgia in the 1990s," in *Contemporary Ukraine on the Cultural Map of Europe*, ed. Larissa M. L. Zaleska Onyshkevych and Maria Rewakowicz (London: Sharp, 2009), 119–30.
[99] Stasiuk, *Dukla*, 111.
[100] Ibid., 54.

lie down and are overtaken by the past, while the future ceases to be of interest, [...].'[101]

But the resurrection of Amalia and her sarcophagus, located in the church of Mary Magdalene, as well as the narrator's erotic view of her can be also seen as an opposition between artlessness and immorality. It is one of many opposing pairs which are represented in the text: religiosity and secularism, spirituality and materiality, imagination and reality. This oppositions continue the opposition between East and West and are interconnected through the (post-)galician space. Further the story of Maria Amalia Mniszchowa is 'a story built around the theme of an unruly nobility that for the most part resisted any and all forms of modernization (including the establishment of a centralized state authority)'[102] which symbolizes the peripheral and immobile nature of this space.

Stasiuk's Personal Galicia: Constructing a Private Geography

However, Stasiuk's Galician space is primarily dominated by private geography and memory which is always bound to the space. 'And I keep going back to Dukla [...]'[103]—the narrator, who can be regarded as Stasiuk's alter ego, declares many times in the story *Dukla* (1997). Stasiuk's story relates the impressions and reflections during his many trips to the small town. These are not only characterized by classical nostalgia, but also through melancholy and mourning, which are both elements of nostalgia[104] and create the story's specific atmosphere. *Dukla* is composed of many fragments of metaphysical observations and memories. Time with all its dimensions has a pivotal role for the narrator.

This space activates nostalgia for his own childhood and youth, his grandparents, a slower time, a sense that is embedded in an area of old

---

[101] Ibid., 74.
[102] Terrence O'Keeffe, "Flight into Light and Darkness-Andrzej Stasiuk's Travel Essays," in *Polish Review* 57/3 (2012): 88.
[103] Stasiuk, *Dukla*, 20.
[104] Boym, *Future of Nostalgia*, 55.

Galicia, which stands for all that is gone but still exists, at least, in memory. What Stasiuk also constructs with his poetics is a mythologized space of Galicia and the narrator's past. Magdalena Marszałek calls the text a 'myth-biography,' which is characterized by three aspects: the description of childhood initialization processes, the embedding in a concrete space as well as metafiction as a literary strategy of the biography. All these aspects are contained in *Dukla*.[105] In this (post-)Galician space the narrator finds all the layers of time: the past, the present, and the future, which is represented by all the possibilities the individual appropriation of the past offers. So, the memories bound to the space are handed down to the next generations through the text in a mythologizing way: a way that is typical for Galicia's heritage.[106] Imagination and reality stand as a paradigm for the past, which is the object of longing, and the present, which is the reason for the narrator's longing. This can be also seen in the narrator's contrasting perceptions of his first love and his grandparents, whom he used to visit in the countryside during his childhood.

The grandfather is characterized as a hard-working and strict man in constant motion. His deep faith as well as the masses and litanies organized by him in his house with the older women of the village created for the first time the feeling of a contradiction in the grandson: 'I felt I had been betrayed by reality.'[107] For the first time he feels the contrast between materiality and spirituality, reality and imagination. The grandmother combines these two opposing spheres with each other. She connects the past with the present as well as life with death by seeing ghosts and talking unemotionally about these experiences, as if they were part of everyday world: 'Her friends and relatives were simply visiting her. They came from

---

[105] Magdalena Marszałek, "Das Phantasma Galizien in der Prosa Andrzej Stasiuk's," in *Stereotyp und Geschichtsmythos in Kunst und Sprache*, ed. Katrin Berwanger and Peter Kosta (Frankfurt am Main: Peter Lang, 2005), 491–493.

[106] For Galicia as a mythos in Polish literature in particular see: Ewa Wiegandt, *Austria Felix, czyli o micie Galicji w polskiej prozie współczesnej* (Poznań: Wydawnictwo Naukowe UAM, 1988); Alois Woldan, *Der Österreich-Mythos in der polnischen Literatur* (Wien: Böhlau, 1996); And in general see: *Mythos Galizien,* ed. Jacek Purchla, Wolfgang Kos et al. (Wien: Wien Museum, 2015).

[107] Stasiuk, *Dukla*, 69.

the past.'[108] Again the past makes its appearance: the narrator is confronted for the first time with death through the passing of his grandmother, turns out not to be final for him, because she survives in her stories: 'and I had the feeling, that this death, and maybe death in general, was somehow, how shall I put it, overrated. I felt that my grandmother was only partially gone. [...] In other words, I knew she was alive.'[109] His grandmother thus lives on in memory and perhaps even beyond. This contrasts stand in one line with the oppositions of East and West which Stasiuk is trying to breach during his travels. Like his negotiations between East and West, also these memories of his private life re-emerge again and again during his stays in Dukla: 'So. I'm standing by the park wall in Dukla and practicing the cult of the ancestors,'[110] notes the narrator. The specific location revives the memories.

Between East and West: Europe's Non-Places

Stasiuk's 'Middle Europe' is further defined by certain non-places which are also constructed through the opposition to the Post-Soviet East and the capitalist West. They dominate his perceptions of Galicia as well as his imagined 'Middle Europe' that emerges also from the individual biographies of its inhabitants:

> After a few years of living in this region I begin to understand, why I came here. It was the instinct of the Middle European plain [...] I have always felt this continuous draught, this continuous draft coming from the East to the West and back. Sometimes it has the literary figure of real wind, sometimes it assumes an metaphorical open shape, of unlimited depths, to finally become a little bit more specific as an wind of history with an incredibly foreseeable course: in this or the other direction, but always through here.[111]

Stasiuk constructs 'Middle Europe' as an abyss oscillating between East and West. A space defined through ambivalences, making them visible and forming new shapes out of them: 'To live in the center means to live

---

[108] Ibid., 96.
[109] Ibid., 97.
[110] Ibid., 98.
[111] Stasiuk, "Dziennik okrętowy," 80.

nowhere.'[112] A different 'nowhere' is characterized by Karl Schlögel: 'In front of our eyes we have non-places: places that have vanished, [...] of these nothing is left besides memory. There is no history in 'nowhere.' [...] Every history has a place.'[113] Stasiuk's travels and texts circle around this 'nowheres' from Schlögel's definition. Stasiuk concentrates on these peripheral, forgotten non-places and gives them a history, so they can become places again. He fears that all the space will follow the unifying pattern of the center: 'Yes, my Euro City of tomorrow will go from nowhere to nowhere.'[114] Stasiuk wants to counteract this dystopia, by embedding the places in his texts, filling them with stories from the individual and collective present and past. In *Dukla* (1997) he returns again and again into this little Polish town from the title and fills it with meaning by referring to the city as special space itself, but also to different historical persons living there centuries ago.[115] *Dukla* is often referred to as the most poetic of his books and was his first work which dealt extensively with travels and Galicia. In Poland, the story is widely regarded as the author's most outstanding achievement,[116] an opinion the author himself seems to have held.[117] In *Opowieści galicyjskie* (1996) [*Tales of Galicia*] he focuses on a village also in the Lower Beskids which was dominated through the PGR (Państwowe Gospodarstwo Rolne, State Agricultural Farm) during the times of the Polish People's Republic. The lives of the inhabitants focused on around this State Agricultural Farm: 'The reality of the PGR was a cosmos. Here you are born, live and die.'[118] In the 1990s the inhabitants seek to look for a new meaning of life, but not everyone finds it. The PGR cosmos turns into the capitalist chaos. Stasiuk brings the story of this people

---

[112] Ibid., 85.
[113] Karl Schlögel, "Spatial turn, endlich," in *Im Raume lesen wir die Zeit*, 71.
[114] Stasiuk, "Dziennik okrętowy," 117.
[115] See: Magdalena Baran-Szołtys and Olena Dvoretska, "Das letzte galizische Territorium. Die Städte Dukla und Stanislau in den Werken von Andrzej Stasiuk und Jurij Andruchovyč," in *Jahrbuch des Wissenschaftlichen Zentrums der Polnischen Akademie der Wissenschaften in Wien* (Wien: PAN, 2016), 179–211.
[116] Bill Johnston, "Introduction," in *Dukla*, Andrzej Stasiuk. Transl. by Bill Johnston (Champaign et al: Dalkey Archive Press, 2011), 7.
[117] "Andrzej Stasiuk," Culture.pl, http://culture.pl/en/artist/andrzej-stasiuk (February 22, 2017)
[118] Stasiuk, *Opowieści galicyjskie*, 6.

forgotten by the new system into literature and gives them meaning. The book also had also a successful screen adaptation: *Wino truskawkowe* (2008) [*Strawberry Wine*] by Dariusz Jabłoński.

Stasiuk's 'nowheres' have two meanings. First, his Middle European 'non-places' in the understanding of Schlögel, second, places like Warsaw, Berlin, Wien, Frankfurt am' Main, which for Stasiuk are all the same, resembling Augé's non-places, present but 'unreal and virtual'[119]: 'Every time I am thinking about Western Europe, I think »glass«. Nothing else comes to my mind.'[120] Over the years the Middle European 'nowheres' were commercialized, changing their meaning slowly from Schlögel's to Augé's definition.[121] Stasiuk's 'Euro City' represents the neoliberal dominance also in this region. At the same time this 'Euro City' verifies the existence of the Middle European nowhere. The following example makes it even clearer:

> Making the laundry lately, I had this sudden brainstorm, that I am a Middle European. Maybe it was the detergent OMO, Ariel, or maybe something else in a colorful box. A distant, half-mythical civilization—maybe Procter and Gamble, or Henkel, or maybe Lever—spoke to me in my mother tongue. More than that, they spoke also to all the other Middle Europeans in their mother tongues: *Praci prostriedok pre farebnú bielizeň. Fékezett habzású mosópor szines ruhakra. Detergent pentru rufe colorate. Proszek do prania tkanin kolorowych* ... [...] I felt that my existence was recognized in a deep and irrevocable way. I looked at other packaging in my bathroom. Toothpastes, deodorants, detergents, and cleaning milks, and from everywhere they announced my Middle European resurrection.[122]

This cynical 'Middle European resurrection' is symptomatic of the replacement of spirituality or religious cult by commerce, parallel to the replacement of the PGR cosmos by the capitalist chaos in *Opowieści galicyjskie*. At another passage in *Dziennik okrętowy* Stasiuk makes it even more visible through the connection between Middle European old women and the Western TV program. Here the West becomes 'virtual' not only in

---

[119] Stasiuk, "Dziennik okrętowy," 118.
[120] Ibid.,119.
[121] For Augé's non-places in Stasiuk's works see: Elisabeth Tropper, "Das neue Europa und seine Nicht(s)-Orte. Gekreuzte Perspektiven in Theatertexten von David Greig, Andrzej Stasiuk und Carles Batlle i Jordà," *Germanica* 56/1 (2015): 95–110.
[122] Stasiuk, "Dziennik okrętowy," 111.

a metaphorical sense. The opposition between East and West becomes visible in the opposition between spirituality and commerce. Middle Europe takes on a new shape through a conjunction of both. Religion gets a new form, it is being slowly replaced by commerce and mixes up with it:

> Old women are watching the world in television. HBO, Hallmark, Discovery, TNT, Planete, Canal+, RTL, [...] overcomes the darkness and frost like the wind. [...] This picture has always fascinated me: "masters of wrestling", "extreme sports magazine", "surfing giants" idle around in the kitchen air, somewhere in Konkova, somewhere in Vapenik, in Pányok or Antonivka, and through the pupils of the eyes come inside the mind of a seventy-year-old woman. They mix up with litanies, prayers, with memories of foreign armies, mix up with memories of times when from spring until late autumn one went around town without shoes, with memories of poverty [...] with chicken broth during holidays and cheese, bread and milk during the whole year, in which the names do not mean any change, but only the merciless passage, and as it was at the beginning, now and always for ever and ever amen.[123]

This feature is even more present in *Dukla* where Stasiuk describes Pope John Paul II's visit to the town. Materiality and spirituality turn more and more into a conjoined contradiction, which can be seen in the 'materialization of holiness.'[124] The festivities for the Pope's visit become a commercialized funfair. Mass consumption with different brands and proper names becomes a feature of the present day and the 'hyperreal West.'[125] Stasiuk tries to achieve a similar effect in the text through massed sequences of quotes, brand names etc.:

> [...] the poor life, cheap crap or wholesale stuff, [...] the Virgin Mary, crystal, gleaming shelves carrying *Chronicle of the Twentieth Century* [...] crystal-clear displays of time and function, air fresheners in johns, linoleum, a Sacred Heart in a rococo frame, a black Panasonic, "extended payment plan available", "St. Christopher, pray for us", [...] Sunday gleam of auto bodywork outside the church, bracelets, chains, Consul aftershave, Samson aftershave, [...] solemnity, satiety, as it was in the beginning, is now, and forever will be, glamour, Moorish arches, a cow right outside, drywall, cheap Popularny cigarettes, porn, hymns, the Feast of Our Lady's Assumption and of Our Lady of the Sowing, itsy-bitsy teeny-weeny tiny polka-dot bikini, Come Holy spirit—the world is a skipping-rope rhyme.[126]

---

[123] Ibid., 95–96.
[124] Stasiuk, *Dukla*, 91.
[125] Stasiuk, "Dziennik okrętowy," 136.
[126] Stasiuk, *Dukla*, 92.

By putting everyday objects, brands of international corporations and prayers next to each other, he puts them on the same plane. This juxtaposition without comment creates a whole cosmos of commerce. If one compares the opposition of materiality and spirituality with the opposition of East and West, Stasiuk's 'Middle Europe' resolves in a 'materialization of holiness,' which for Stasiuk constitutes 'the secret of the human soul, especially the Middle European soul, whose existence was never really proven, but whose reality was never really disproved.'[127] This disbanding of the East-West-opposition is accompanied by permanent criticism towards globalization which leads to a unification of all geographical and mental spaces and robs all of them of their individuality.

Moving through Immovable Spaces

'Travel is always an escape and it works like a drug. [...] Tell me what you have left and I tell you, who you are,'[128] states Stasiuk characterizing his own desire to travel. Although he calls himself a 'Middle European', he defines the 'Middle Europeans' in contrast to himself as settled and he outlines why. They bound themselves to material objects or land as an escape from unstable reality that in this region is so deeply threatened by historical events: 'Surely this is a utopia. I just look for passages to cross on the other side of the picture, vanished places in a regular tangle of landscapes and travels. This is a Middle European disease, a tactic of suspicion against reality.'[129] 'The world is a fiction,'[130] Stasiuk writes and illustrates 'Middle Europe' as a space of distrust of history, borders, homeland, and stability:

> That is why Middle Europe never gave birth to any great travelers. She was busy travelling her own insides. To be on the road just out of curiosity? An idea like this can only come into somebody's mind who is sure of the inviolability of his own house, to somebody, who does not worry about his home standing still at the same

---

[127] Stasiuk, "Dziennik okrętowy," 96.
[128] Ibid., 117–118.
[129] Ibid., 131.
[130] Ibid., 97.

place when he comes back. It is possible, that this ostentatious settlement, this immobility of quarters is coming from the deep feeling of homelessness in a deeper, mental sense. The demon of chaos, the bad ghost of indetermination is creeping in the emptiness separating towns, and that is why the houses stand so close to each other, they look inside each other's windows and in a human way look for one owns reflection—just to make sure it exists.[131]

This quote shows how space dominates over time, which can only be materialized by space: 'because salvation and redemption cannot take place in time, but only in space through the universal reincarnation of matter.'[132] At the same time Stasiuk bounds this settlement to movement that in this region was always forced: expulsions, resettlements, flights, mass migrations, especially in the twentieth century. These movements stick on to this land just like the settlement. This is just another opposition of 'Middle Europe.' This complex space with its chronotopical character is defining Stasiuk's poetics. His 'Middle Europe' and his Galicia are anti-historical, concentrating on geography and space, because they make time evident: 'This is happening, because geography is my obsession, never history, whose huge, half-dead and bad bulk has fed us in this lands for so long. But geography was given to us like a revelation, and it is one of the few things we weren't able to fuck up.'[133] This geography focuses only on real space and isolates oneself from political, economic topographies, which are called 'bastards'[134] in the text.

At the same time these topics are mentioned all the time, as I showed through the previous examples demonstrating the East / West opposition. Stasiuk's poetics seems to be a contradiction in itself. He does not do what he preaches. He seduces the reader and betrays him, but on the other hand, he never promised he would do it differently. His poetics was always based on fiction and imagination, even in political topics like 'Middle Europe.' Concerning the contradiction between fictional and non-fictional literature Stasiuk expands on in an interview:

---

[131] Ibid., 101.
[132] Ibid., 94.
[133] Ibid., 120.
[134] Ibid., 120.

I am not an expert. I do not deal with reportages, anyway I do not even read them, they bore me. In it you can find the so-called "truth", which really does not bother me at all. Lies are more interesting. The personal relation is more interesting. The reportage wants to be objective that is why it is tasteless, without attributes. People like it, it is a good read, but it is not literature. The world is the basis for hilarious making ups, fantasizing, private illusions, and this is what attracts me, not somewhat of a "truth". I am just making up reality.[135]

Conclusion

Stasiuk's post-Galician space in the context of his imagined 'Middle Europe' defines itself through the peripheral Otherness beyond East and West. This Otherness is well described by Boris Groys: 'Beyond identity and difference lies the sphere of the undifferentiated, indifferent, arbitrary, banal, unremarkable, unappealing, not worth mentioning, non-identical, and indifferent.'[136] Precisely these features characterize Stasiuk's 'Middle Europe.' Trapped in a motionless presence, his space is open to all possibilities: 'everything was ready for the craziest thoughts. So little happened here, that the future opened an endless number of possibilities.'[137] Stasiuk's 'Middle Europe' and Galicia become a microcosm for his own imaginings, based mostly on his own memories. Galicia is a vanished space and is uableable to respond, therefore, the Polish author reconstructs it according to his own wishes. This space is not able to fight back and thus serves as a template for fiction: Stasiuk is making places out of non-places, stories out of missing histories. He describes reality through a lense of his own in which he gives meaning to the meaningless and makes the invisible visible. Therefore, Stasiuk's concept of 'Middle Europe' differs from other conceptualizations through his a-historic, personal and imaginative character. It does not have to be the 'true' Central Europe, it just has to be his 'Middle Europe.' Perhaps this is the unique offering of Middle Europe, namely, the possibility to oscillate between antagonisms, choosing both or

---

[135] Stasiuk, *Życie to jednak strata jest*, 148.
[136] Boris Groys, *Über das Neue. Versuch einer Kulturökonomie* (München, Wien: Carl Hanser, 1992), 48.
[137] Stasiuk, "Dziennik okrętowy," 110.

none, mixing them up, but being unable to escape them. At least this is what Stasiuk's texts reveal.

Abstract

This paper analyses Andrzej Stasiuk's concept of 'Middle Europe' in his texts from the 1990s (*Dziennik okrętowy*, *Dukla*, *Opowieści galicyjskie*) as they were part of a public discourse which has defined Poland's transition after 1989. Drawing on the theoretical concept of geopoetics, this analysis demonstrates how Stasiuk's work oscillates between East and West and creates his own 'Middle Europe' by displaying and utilizing ideas from the mythological concepts of Austrian Galicia (Habsburg Empire), Kresy and Sarmatia. Stasiuk's 'Middle Europe' represents an attempt to overcome the East / West opposition and he relies on the cultural, collective heritage of Galicia, Kresy and Sarmatia. Stasiuk achieves this by connecting these ideas in his private geography, which features imaginary flashbacks to personal memories. Stasiuk's 'Middle Europe' is an empty space which becomes a microcosm for his own imaginations and re-construction.

Keywords: imagined space, non-place, orientalism, East-West distinction, travel literature, travel narratives, travelogues, Kresy, Sarmatia, Austrian Galicia, Habsburg Empire, Middle Europe, Central Europe, contemporary Polish literature, Andrzej Stasiuk

Bibliography

Andruchowycz, Jurij, "Z nienapisanej książki Granice Europy." in *Diabeł tkwi w serze*. Jurij Andruchowycz. Wołowiec: Czarne 2007, 16–21.

Andruchowytsch, Juri, and Andrzej Stasiuk. *Mein Europa. Zwei Essays über das sogenannte Mitteleuropa*. Frankfurt am Main: Suhrkamp 2004.

Bakuła, Bogusław, "Colonial and Postcolonial Aspects of Polish Discourse on the 'Borderlands.'" in *From Sovietology to Postcoloniality. Poland and Ukraine from a Postcolonial Perspective*, ed. Janusz Korek. Stockholm: Södertörn högskola 2007, 41–59.

Bakuła, Bogusław, "Colonial and Postcolonial Aspects of Polish Borderland Studies: An Outline." *Teksty Drugie* 1 (2014): 96–123.

Baran-Szołtys, Magdalena, and Olena Dvoretska, "Das letzte galizische Territorium. Die Städte Dukla und Stanislau in den Werken von Andrzej Stasiuk und Jurij Andruchovyč." in *Jahrbuch des Wissenschaftlichen Zentrums der Polnischen Akademie der Wissenschaften in Wien*. Wien: PAN 2016, 179–211.

Baran-Szołtys, Magdalena, "Visions of the Past: Revised in the Present, Recreated for the Future. Nostalgia for and Travels to Galicia in Polish Literature after 1989." in *Galizien in Bewegung. Wahrnehmungen – Begegnungen – Verflechtungen*, ed. Magdalena Baran-Szołtys, Olena Dvoretska et al. Göttingen: Vienna University Press at V&R unipress 2018, 75–90.

Borkowska, Grażyna, "Perspektywa postkolonialna na gruncie polskim – pytania sceptyka." *Teksty Drugie* 5 (2010): 40–52.

Bömelburg, Hans-Jürgen, and Renate Stößinger et al., ed. *Vertreibungen aus dem Osten Deutsche und Polen erinnern sich*. Olsztyn: Borussia 2000.

Boym, Svetlana. *The Future of Nostalgia*. New York: Basic Books 2001.

Cytacka, Agnieszka, "Nie wiadomo, po co się jedzie. Z Andrzejem Stasiukiem rozmawia Agnieszka Cytacka." *Czytanie Literatury* 4 (2015): 237–248.

Czaplińska, Maria, "Mniszchowa z Brühlów Maria Amelia." in *Polski Słownik Biograficzny*, Vol. 21, ed. Emanuel Rostworski. Wrocław et al.: PAN / PAU,1976, 452–454.

Dubasevych, Roman, "Über Erinnerung in der Postmoderne. Paradigmen der westukrainischen Literatur nach der Wende." in *Galizien. Fragmente eines diskursiven Raums*, ed. Doktoratskolleg Galizien. Innsbruck et al.: Studien Verlag 2009, 197–227.

Frank, Susi K., "Geokulturologie – Geopoetik. Definitions- und Abgrenzungsvorschläge." in *Geopoetiken. Geographische Entwürfe in den mittel- und osteuropäischen Literaturen*, ed. Magdalena Marszałek and Sylvia Sasse. Berlin: Kadmos 2010, 19–42.

Gnauck, Gerhard, "Der Ruf der Beskiden." *Neue Zürcher Zeitung*, August 16 (2012), www.nzz.ch/feuilleton/buecher/der-ruf-der-beskiden-1.17482029 (acc. 09.04.2016).

Golec, Janusz. *Od Wiednia do Czerniowiec. Galicja i Bukowina w wybranych niemieckojęzycznych utworach literackich*. Lublin: Wydawnictwo Uniwersytetu Marii Curie-Skłodowskiej 2017.

Gosk, Hanna, "Postcolonial or Postdependency Studies." *Teksty Drugie* 1 (2014): 235–247.

Groys, Boris. *Über das Neue. Versuch einer Kulturökonomie*. München, Wien: Carl Hanser 1992.

Haid, Elisabeth, Stephanie Weismann et al., "Einleitung." in *Galizien. Peripherie der Moderne – Moderne der Peripherie?*. ed. Elisabeth Haid, Stephanie Weismann et al. Marburg: Herder 2013, 1–10.

Jagodzinski, Sabine, "Mit den Waffen des Gegners – Orientalische Elemente und Gedenken der Türkenkriege in der polnischen Adelskultur des 17. Jhs." in *Sarmatismus versus Orientalismus in Mitteleuropa / Sarmatyzm versus Orientalizm w Europie Środkowej*, ed. Magdalena Długosz and Piotr O. Scholz with the assistance of Martin Faber. Berlin: Frank & Timme 2012, 315–353.

Janion, Maria, "Sarmaci na pograniczu." in *Niesamowita Słowiańszczyzna. Fantazmaty literatury,* Maria Janion. Kraków: Wydawnictwo Literackie 2007, 176–179.

Johnston, Bill, "Introduction." in *Dukla,* Andrzej Stasiuk. Translated by Bill Johnston. Champaign et al: Dalkey Archive Press 2011.

Kieniewicz, Stefan, "Kresy. Przemiany terminologiczne w perspektywie dziejowej." *Przegląd Wschodni* 1 (1991): 3–13.

Kliems, Alfrun, "Aggressiver Lokalismus: Undergroundästhetik, Antiurbanismus und Regionsbehauptung bei Andrzej Stasiuk und Jurij Andruchovyč." *Zeitschrift für Slawistik* 56/2 (2011): 197–213.

Kolbuszewski, Jacek. *Kresy*. Wrocław: Wydawnictwo Dolnośląskie 1995.

Kolbuszewski, Jacek, "Kresy – pojęcie, znaczenia, wartości." in *Kresowe dziedzictwo. Studia nad językiem, historią i kulturą,* ed. Anna Burzyńska-Kamienicka and Małgorzata Misiak. Wrocław: ATUT 2012, 11–23.

Kołodziejczyk, Dorota, "Postkolonialny transfer na Europę Środkowo-Wschodnią." *Teksty Drugie* 5 (2010): 22–39.

Koper, Sławomir. *Spacer po Lwowie. Przewodnik po Kresach*. Warszawa: Axel Springer 2008.

Kowal, Grzegorz, "Mit(y) Galicji." in *Pogranicza, Kresy, Wschód a idee Europy*, ed. Anna Janicka, Grzegorz Kowalski et al. Białystok: Książnica Podlaska im. Łukasza Górnickiego 2013, 609–652.

Kowalczyk, Jerzy, "Die Bedeutung des wettinischen Königshofes für den kulturellen und künstlerischen Austausch – Polen in Sachsen, Sachsen in Polen." in *Die Personalunionen von Sachsen-Polen 1697–1763 und Hannover-England 1714–1837. Ein Vergleich*, ed. Rex Rexheuser. Wiesbaden: Harrassowitz 2005, 201–220.

Kożuchowski, Adam, and Werner Nell, "Galizien. Zerrissene und wiedergefundene Geschichten." in *Deutsch-Polnische Erinnerungsorte. Geteilt / Gemeinsam*, ed. Hans Henning Hahn and Robert Traba. Paderborn: Ferdinand Schöningh 2015, 177–196.

Kundera, Milan, "The Tragedy of Central Europe." Trans. by Edmund White. *New York Review of Books* 31/7 (April 26, 1984): 3–38.

Kundera, Milan, "Un Occident kidnappé ou la tragédie de l'Europe centrale." *Le Débat* 27 (1983): 3–22.

Lipiński, Krzysztof, "Die 'Habsburgische Atlantis' in Galizien." in *Galizien als gemeinsame Literaturlandschaft*, ed. Fridrun Rinner and Klaus Zerinschek. Innsbruck: Institut für Sprachwissenschaft 1988, 55–64.

Maciejewski, Janusz, "Sarmatyzm jako formacja kulturowa." *Teksty* 4 (1974): 13–42

Marszałek, Magdalena, "Das Phantasma Galizien in der Prosa Andrzej Stasiuk's." in *Stereotyp und Geschichtsmythos in Kunst und Sprache*, ed. Katrin Berwanger and Peter Kosta. Frankfurt am Main: Peter Lang 2005, 485–498.

Marszałek, Magdalena, "'Pamięć, meteorologia oraz urojenia': środkowoeuropejska geopoetyka Andrzeja Stasiuka." in *Literatura, kultura i język polski w kontekstach i kontaktach światowych*, ed. Małgorzata Czermińska and Katarzyna Meller et al. Poznań: Wydawnictwo Naukowe Uniwersytetu im. Adama Mickiewicza 2007.

Marszałek, Magdalena, "Anderes Europa. Zur (ost)mitteleuropäischen Geopoetik." in *Geopoetiken. Geographische Entwürfe in den mittel- und osteuropäischen Literaturen,* ed. Magdalena Marszałek and Sylvia Sasse. Berlin: Kadmos 2010, 43–67.

Marszałek, Magdalena, "Der Schriftsteller als Geograph und Gastarbeiter: Die literarische Kartographie Andrzej Stasiuks." *Germanoslavica. Zeitschrift für germano-slavische Studien* 21/1–2 (2010): 146–156.

Naumann, Friedrich. *Mitteleuropa.* Berlin: Reimer 1915.

Niedźwiedź, Jakub, "Sarmatyzm, czyli tradycja wynaleziona." *Teksty Drugie* 1 (2015): 46–62.

Nowicka, Ewa, and Aleksandra Bilewicz. *Pamięć utraconych ojczyzn.* Warszawa: Wydawnictwo Uniwersytetu Warszawskiego 2012.

O'Keeffe, Terrence, "Flight into Light and Darkness-Andrzej Stasiuk's Travel Essays." *Polish Review* 57/3 (2012): 83–99.

Orłowicz, Mieczysław. *Ilustrowany przewodnik po Galicji, Bukowinie, Spiszu, Orawie i Śląsku Cieszyńskim.* Lviv: Akademicki Klub Turystyczny w Lwowie 1919, 380–384.

Olszewski, Michał, "Eseje o równowadze (Jurij Andruchowycz, Andrzej Stasiuk – 'Moja Europa')." *Studium* 5–6 (2000): 130–135.

Partsch, Joseph. *Mitteleuropa. Die Länder und Völker von den Westalpen und dem Balkan bis an den Kanal und das Kurische Haff.* Ghota: Perthes 1904.

Pol, Wincenty. *Mohort. Rapsod rycerski z podania.* Warszawa: M. Arct 1909.

Purchla, Jacek, Wolfgang Kos et al., ed. *Mythos Galizien.* Wien, Kraków: Wien Museum, 2015.

Purchla, Jacek, "Ein Galizien nach Galizien. Über den einzigartigen Mythos von einem 'verschwundenen Königreich.'" in *Mythos Galizien,* ed. Jacek Purchla, Wolfgang Kos et al. Wien, Kraków: Wien Museum 2015, 49–53.

Rinner, Fridrun, and Klaus Zerinschek, ed. *Galizien als gemeinsame Literaturlandschaft.* Innsbruck: Institut für Sprachwissenschaft 1988.

Said, Edward. *Orientalism.* New York: Pantheon Books 1978.

Sid, Igor', and the group Poluostrov, "Osnovnoy vopros geopoetiki." Pervay a konferentsiya po geopoetike (Moskva, Krymskiy klub, 24.04.1996), http://liter.net/geopoetics/penin.html (acc. 21.02.2017).

Schimsheimer, Christof, "Die Galizische Geschichte: zur Reproduktion literarischer und historischer Narrative am Beispiel von Andrzej Stasiuks Prosa." in *Galizien als Kultur- und Gedächtnislandschaft im kultur- und sprachwissenschaftlichen Diskurs*, ed. Ruth Büttner and Anna Hanus. Frankfurt am Main: Peter Lang 2015, 261–281.

Schimsheimer, Christof, "Galicia and the Kresy as Polish Places of Memory in Comparison." in *Galizien in Bewegung. Wahrnehmungen – Begegnungen – Verflechtungen*, ed. Magdalena Baran-Szołtys, Olena Dvoretska et al. Göttingen: Vienna University Press at V&R unipress 2018, 37–55.

Schlögel, Karl, "Karten monochrom: der Nationalstaat." in *Im Raume lesen wir die Zeit*. Karl Schlögel. München: Hanser 2003, 199–210.

Schlögel, Karl, "Lehrstück I. Fall der Berliner Mauer 1989." in *Im Raume lesen wir die Zeit*. Karl Schlögel. München: Hanser 2003, 25–35.

Schlögel, Karl, "Spatial turn, endlich.' in *Im Raume lesen wir die Zeit*. Karl Schlögel. München: Hanser 2003, 60–71.

Stasiuk, Andrzej. *Opowieści galicyjskie*. Kraków: Znak 1995.

Stasiuk, Andrzej. *Tales of Galicia*. Translated by Margarita Nafpaktitis. Prague: Twisted Spoon Press 2003.

Stasiuk, Andrzej. *Biały kruk*. Poznań: Biblioteka Czasu Kultury 1995.

Stasiuk, Andrzej. *Przez rzekę*. Gładyszów: Czarne 1996.

Stasiuk, Andrzej. *Dukla*. Gładyszów: Czarne 1997.

Stasiuk, Andrzej, "Dziennik okrętowy." in *Moja Europa. Dwa eseje o Europie zwanej Środkową*, Jurij Andruchowycz and Andrzej Stasiuk. Wołowiec: Czarne 2000, 83–157.

Stasiuk, Andrzej. *Tekturowy samolot*. Wołowiec: Czarne 2000.

Stasiuk, Andrzej. *Zima i inne opowiadania*. Wołowiec: Czarne 2001.

Stasiuk, Andrzej. *Jadąc do Babadag*. Wołowiec: Czarne 2004.

Stasiuk, Andrzej. *Fado*. Wołowiec: Czarne 2006.

Stasiuk, Andrzej. *Dziennik pisany później.* Wołowiec: Czarne 2010.

Stasiuk, Andrzej. *Wschód.* Wołowiec: Czarne 2014.

Stasiuk, Andrzej, and Dorota Wodecka. *Życie to jednak strata jest.* Wołowiec: Czarne 2015.

Stasiuk, Andrzej. *Osiołkem.* Wołowiec: Czarne 2016.

Stefanowska, Lidia, "Back to the Golden Age: the Discourse of Nostalgia in the 1990s." in *Contemporary Ukraine on the Cultural Map of Europe*, ed. Larissa M. L. Zaleska Onyshkevych and Maria Rewakowicz. London: Sharp 2009, 119–30.

Suleja, Włodzimierz, "Trudny proces zakorzenienia. Kresowiacy na Dolnym Śląsku." in *Kresowe dziedzictwo. Studia nad językiem, historią i kulturą*, ed. Anna Burzyńska-Kamienicka, Małgorzata Misiak et al. Wrocław: ATUT 2012, 269–275.

Swieykowski, Emmanuel. *Monografia Dukli, Studya do historyi sztuki i kultury wieku osiemnastego w Polsce.* Kraków: Akademia umiejętności 1903.

Syrnyk, Jarosław. *Ludność ukraińska na Dolnym Śląsku (1945–1989).* Wrocław: IPN 2007.

Tropper, Elisabeth, "Das neue Europa und seine Nicht(s)-Orte. Gekreuzte Perspektiven in Theatertexten von David Greig, Andrzej Stasiuk und Carles Batlle i Jordà." *Germanica* 56/1 (2015): 95–110.

Uffelmann, Dirk, "'Here you have all my stuff!' Real Things from a Mythical Country: Ottoman 'Sarmatica' in Enlightened Poland." in *Präsenz und Evidenz fremder Dinge im Europa des 18. Jahrhunderts, ed.* Birgit Neumann. Göttingen: Wallstein 2015, 323–338.

Walder, Dennis, "Remembering Rousseau. Nostalgia and the Responsibilities of the Self." *Third World Quarterly* 26/3 (2005): 423–430.

Wedemann, Marek, "Gdzie leży Beresteczko? Kresy na mapie." in *Kresy. Dekonstrukcja*, ed. Krzysztof Trybuś, Jerzy Kałążny et al. Poznań: Poznańskie Towarzystwo Przyjaciół Nauk Redakcja Wydawnictw 2007, 11–35.

Weretiuk, Oksana, "Jurij Andruchowycz i Andrzej Stasiuk o tożsamości ukształtowanej przez historię." *Porównania* 9 (2011): 89–100.

Wiącek, Elżbieta, and Karolina Golemo, "Galicja for ever – nostalgiczny sen o utraconej Arkadii, moda na monarchię czy atrakcja turystyczna?" in *Semiotyczna mapa Małopolski*, ed. Elżbieta Wiącek. Kraków: Ksiegarnia Akademicka 2015, 141–223.

Wierzejska, Jagoda, "Mit południa jako kontrapunkt dla opozycji Wschód-Zachód i podstawa mitu Europy Środkowej." *Porównania* 11 (2012): 71–86.

Wierzejska, Jagoda, "(Post-)bordering Galicia in Ukrainian and Polish Post-colonial Discourse: The Cases of Yurii Andrukhovych and Andrzej Stasiuk." in *Journal of European Studies* 47, no. 2 (2017): 174–189.

Wierzejska, Jagoda, "Central European Palimpsests: Postcolonial Discourse in Works by Andrzej Stasiuk and Yurii Andrukhovych." in *Postcolonial Europe? Essays on Post-Communism Literatures and Cultures*, ed. Dobrota Pucherová and Róbert Gáfrik. Leiden, Boston: Koninklijke Brill 2015, 375–397.

White, Kenneth, "An Outline of Geopoetics." The International Institute of Geopoetics, http://institut-geopoetique.org/en/articles-en/37-an-outline-of-geopoetics (acc. 10.11.2017).

Wolff, Larry, "Inventing Galicia. Messianic Josephinism and the Recasting of Partitioned Poland." *Slavic Review* 63/3 (2004): 818–840.

Wolff, Larry. *The Idea of Galicia. History and Fantasy in Habsburg Political Culture*. Stanford: Stanford University Press 2010.

Wiegandt, Ewa. *Austria Felix, czyli o micie Galicji w polskiej prozie współczesnej*. Poznań: Wydawnictwo Naukowe Uniwersytetu im. Adama Mickiewicza 1988.

Woldan, Alois. *Der Österreich-Mythos in der polnischen Literatur*. Wien: Böhlau 1996.

Woldan, Alois, "Nachwort." in *Europa erlesen. Galizien*. ed. Stefan Simonek and Alois Woldan. Klagenfurt: Wieser 1998, 203–207.

Internet Sources

Culture.pl. "Andrzej Stasiuk." Accessed February 22, 2017. http://culture.pl/en/artist/andrzej-stasiuk

Czarne. Accessed April 9, 2016. http://czarne.com.pl/

Nike Nagroda Literacka. "Nike 2016." Accessed February 21, 2017. http://www.nike.org.pl/strona.php?p=29&eid=23

Serwis informacyjny Gminy Dukla. "Dane statystyczne." Accessed November 9, 2017. http://www.dukla.pl/gmina_okolice.php?no=5.

Serwis informacyjny Gminy Dukla. "Miejscowości Gminy Dukla." Accessed November 9, 2017. http://www.dukla.pl/gmina_okolice.php?no=4

Mariella C. Gronenthal

LONGING FOR THE EMPTY SPACE— NOSTALGIA AND CENTRAL EUROPE

> If I were to think of a coat of arms for Central Europe, I would put semidarkness into one half, and emptiness into the other. The first as a sign of non-evidence, the second as a sign for the space as of yet untamed. A beautiful coat of arms with somewhat indistinct outlines that can be filled with imagination. Or dreams.[1]

In his essay *Logbook*, Andrzej Stasiuk drafts his own idea of a Central Europe, by creating a fictitious coat of arms. As intriguing as it may seem to visualize an ambivalent concept such as this, Stasiuk draws upon a somewhat problematic imagery. According to his poetic heraldry, two notions symbolize Central Europe: semidarkness and emptiness. While the former suggests that something undisclosed might be at stake, the latter postulates a lack of existence as such. Both terms—and referring to them as 'terms' is more suitable than as 'images' due to a difficult perception as actual visual configurations—have an important common denominator: They invite the reader to project his own imagined geography, topography or (cultural) iconography of Central Europe onto them. Central Europe, then, is a blank screen for projections, for attributions that can be of a highly subjective and emotional nature.

Since the 19th century, the idea of Central Europe has made several discursive journeys from insignificance to its own renaissance and back again.[2] During this time, it has been exploited for varying causes—ranging from the imperial impetus in Friedrich Naumann to the anti-imperial polemic of Milan Kundera.[3] This versatile instrumentalization of the concept

---

[1] Andrzej Stasiuk, "Dziennik Okrętowy," in *Moja Europa. Dwa eseje o Europie zwanej Środkową,* Jurij Andruchowycz and Andrzej Stasiuk (Wołowiec: Czarne 2001), 102. All translations from Polish and German, unless otherwise specified, by the author of this article, MCG.

[2] A well-written overview can be found in: Matthias Rüb, "Wo liegt Mitteleuropa?" *Kafka – Zeitschrift für Mitteleuropa* 1, no. 1 (2001): 14–21.

[3] See Friedrich Naumann, *Mitteleuropa*. (Berlin: Reimer, 1915); Milan Kundera, "The Tragedy of Central Europe," trans. by Edmund White. *New York Review of Books*,

affirms Stasiuk's construction of Central Europe as a projection screen which leaves room for cultural, political and historical ideas of varying provenance. Central Europe in this sense is a political means rather than a definite and definable space.

Figure 17: People of Silesia (1932). Public Domain.

This way of imagining Central Europe shows remarkable structural parallels to reconstructing the past in nostalgic memories—nostalgia works by perceiving deficiencies in the present and projecting the fulfillment of this void onto a certain time of the past. The past, then, can also be a vague and unclear space and, in its nostalgic imagination, can become object to projections of idyllic peace and material well-being. The aim of this essay is

---

26.04.1984: 33–38. Karl Schlögel has observed this ambivalence in his essay "Die Mitte liegt ostwärts. Die Deutschen, der verlorene Osten und Mitteleuropa" [1986]. In: Karl Schlögel, *Die Mitte liegt ostwärts. Europa im Übergang* (Frankfurt am Main: Fischer 2008), 16.

to pursue the connections between Central Europe and nostalgia and to test the fruitfulness of their mutual influence.[4]

Central Europe is strongly defined by its history,[5] thus, it must be understood as a target of projection in both its spatial and its temporal dimensions. Therefore it is the perfect object for nostalgic memories. It is, in fact, impossible to speak of Central Europe without mentioning the imperial powers that have shaped its history, namely the Austro-Hungarian Empire, the Russian Empire, the Ottoman Empire and, to a lesser degree, the second German Empire. It is especially the Habsburg Monarchy which gives grounds for nostalgic reflections on a Central European past, for example in Yurii Andrukhovych, who uses the topos of Austro-Hungarian Galicia to inscribe (Western) Ukraine onto a Central European discourse.[6]

Moreover, Galicia is but one example for Central Europe's specific regionalism.[7] Rather than being a transnational entity, it seems to constitute a conglomerate of regions that defy today's national borders: There is, to name just a few, Bukovina, Silesia, Bohemia and Moravia, Vojvodina, Banat and Transylvania. These historically defined regions with pasts that shape their present local identities entwine space with time. Central Europe as a complex of regions is laden with an intense cultural memory that potentially outweighs its spatial structure. In Central Europe, the diffusion of memory and topography is of a much denser quality than elsewhere. This intertwined space-time-relation is yet another indicator for a nostalgic potential which is deeply inscribed into the ideas of a Central Europe.

---

[4] These and the following observations are to be understood within the context of my PhD dissertation on nostalgia in German and Polish contemporary family novels set during socialism.

[5] Milan Kundera has called it a 'realm inhabited by the same memories, the same problems and conflicts, the same common tradition' . Kundera, "Tragedy," 35.

[6] Cf. Yurii Andrukhovych, *Dezorijentacija na miscevosti. Sproby* (Ivano-Frankivs'k: Lileja-NV, 2006).

[7] Connections to Alfrun Kliems' 'aggressive localism' are not coincidental, cf. Alfrun Kliems, "Aggressiver Lokalismus: Undergroundästhetik, Antiurbanismus und Regionsbehauptung bei Andrzej Stasiuk und Jurij Andruchovyč," *Zeitschrift für Slawistik* 56, no. 2 (2011): 197–213. While her focus is urbanism and underground culture, Kliems also discusses the Central European dimension of the works of Andrzej Stasiuk and Jurij Andruchovyč.

Stasiuk also picks up on this same notion in his aforementioned essay. He reflects on the role of history as such when he talks about the region's fragmented character:

> Yes, this is what my Europe is made out of. Out of peculiarities, out of trifles, out of impressions that last but nanoseconds and that are reminiscent of film studies, out of twinkling scraps that swirl through my head like leaves in the wind, and shining through that drift of episodes are maps and landscapes. This is so, because my obsession has always been geography, never history, whose great, half dead and decaying bulk we have fed on in our regions for so long.[8]

First of all, the 'peculiarities,' the 'trifles' and 'impressions' correspond with the idea of Central Europe not being a homogenous region. Rather, it must be seen as a compilation of regional units that have specific expressions for their mutual experiences and common cultural forms. Furthermore, when Stasiuk focuses on topography, this points the reader to his works *Tales from Galicia*, *Dukla* and *On the Road to Babadag*, all of which are translated into English and refer to the regionalism of Central Europe as well. In these texts he unfolds—through his landscapes—a sort of nostalgic longing.

What is most remarkable about the quote is the treatment of history. Stasiuk creates a specific Central Europe that is made up of landscapes. Even if he admits to the fact that they are shaped predominantly by history, his primary focus lies on the spatial dimensions, however temporally charged they are. However, the metaphor tells us space is dead and thus bound to poison those who feed on it, whereas history is still the main source for intellectual nourishment. It comes as no surprise then that nostalgia is also often modelled as something toxic in post-socialist literature.[9]

Consequently, Central Europe intertwines notions of space and time. Nostalgia is structured similarly as it oscillates between them as well. When Johannes Hofer coined the term in 1688, he derived it mainly from the German *Heimweh* and the French *Maladie du Pays*, also focusing on

---

[8] Stasiuk, "Dziennik," 120.
[9] Examples can be found in: Uwe Tellkamp, *Der Turm* (Frankfurt am Main: Suhrkamp 2008), in which a recurrent motif is the notion of 'sweet sickness yesterday' as a metaphor for nostalgia. As well as in: Joanna Bator, *Piaskowa Góra* (Warszawa: W.A.B. 2009), which will be discussed below.

the spatial dimension.[10] The temporal shift, according to Jean Starobinski, did not appear until the 18th century, when the longing suddenly shifted from 'the actual *place* where [one] passed his childhood but [to] youth itself'.[11] Today, nostalgia is perceived mainly as a longing for the past, yet this past is unintelligible without a space in which it can be configured. This is why the idea of *Heimat* is closely related to nostalgia and together they are a driving force in exile literature. In fact, it is possible to see nostalgic images as chronotopes in the sense of Mikhail Bakhtin[12]—a concept that may also prove fruitful for the different regions of Central Europe.

The final structural parallel between concepts of Central Europe and nostalgic pasts is their relational quality that defines them as in-between spaces. Milan Kundera makes this quite clear when he writes that Central Europe is 'the part of Europe situated geographically in the center—culturally in the West and politically in the East.'[13] Since the Cold War, it has been defined by its relation to its bordering countries and by, quite literally, being caught in the middle. This characteristic has obtained different dimensions in post-socialism when the division of East and West has lost some—although not all—of its political meaning. While previously, the debate had centered on distancing Central Europe from the Soviet sphere, a post-socialist Central Europe separates itself from both the East and the West, as does Stasiuk:

> To be Central European, that is: to live between the East that never existed, and the West that existed all too much. That is, to live 'in the center', when the center is in fact the only real country. Only that this country is not fixed. It is more like an island, maybe a floating one.[14]

---

[10] Johannes Hofer, "Medical Dissertation on Nostalgia by Johannes Hofer, 1688," Trans. by Carolyn Kiser Anspach. *Bulletin of the Institute of the History of Medicine* 2 (1934), 376–391, §2.
[11] Jean Starobinski, "The Idea of Nostalgia," *Diogenes* 14 (1966), 94.
[12] For the concept of the chronotope: cf. Mikhail M. Bakhtin, *The Dialogic Imagination: Four Essays*, Trans. by Caryl Emerson and Michael Holquist (Austin: University of Texas Press, 1994).
[13] Kundera, "Tragedy," 33.
[14] Stasiuk, "Dziennik," 136.

Like Kundera, Stasiuk still defines Central Europe in relation to both the East and the West. Yet the previous desire to belong to the West and leave the East behind has changed into a feeling of peculiarity and singularity, of not belonging to either sphere. Stasiuk also distances himself from a German understanding of Central Europe when he writes: 'Mitteleuropa did not translate into my Central Europe in any way, because it was only an emissary of the hyperreal West.'[15] Here, Central Europe is used to defy both socialism and capitalism, and, ultimately, critique political and economic ideologies as such.

How does this relate to nostalgia? Nostalgia creates emotionally influenced images of the past that rely largely on the perception of the present. They express a desire for a certain distance from the present in favor of belonging to a possibly idealized or romanticized past. In this sense, nostalgia is a figure of distinction, just as much as Central Europe is. It is a longing to remove oneself from the present. At the same time, it does not prove a true desire for the factual past, but rather for a 'Third Space,' an in-between space that is modelled in an image of a past fueled by the present's deficiencies. Remarkably, nostalgia is also utilized to criticize ideology in post-socialist novels. By mentally fleeing into the past, flaws of the present are made abundantly clear. This nostalgically perceived past functions as a sort of escapism and simultaneously heightens the sense for historic experiences that an ideologically contaminated present might wish to forget.

---

[15] Stasiuk, "Dziennik," 135–136.

Gruß aus Eisenau, Krs. Oppeln
Figure 18: Prewar Eisenau in Silesia (1939). Public Domain.

Both an imagined Central Europe and a nostalgically imagined past therefore (1) function as projective screens, (2) intertwine space and time, and (3) dissociate themselves from the present as an ideologically charged reference frame. During the conference which inspired this paper, a recurrent discussion of the market value of the notion of Central Europe took place. The idea that Central Europe can be turned into a lucrative label that is imposed on artists and their works is all the more interesting as nostalgia is still highly controversial. After all, it is usually connoted by pejorative meanings such as falsification, romanticization or belittlement of the past.

Yet the question still stands whether it might be Central Europe's nostalgic potential that speaks to a broad audience and heightens its market value. Examples from Polish post-socialist literature will illustrate these observations clearly. Here, notions of Central Europe and nostalgia are interconnected through projection, chronotopic quality and critique of the present in the motif of the so-called Eastern 'Borderlands.'[16] The term describes areas in today's Lithuania, Belarus and Ukraine that Poland lost to the Soviet Union after World War II when it was moved West on the map and gained formerly German regions. The loss of these areas inspires different narratives in Polish history and influences even today's configurations of the Polish nation. Namely, Inga Iwasiów's novel *Bambino* (2008) and Joanna Bator's novel *Sand Mountain* [*Piaskowa Góra*] (2009) make use of the 'Borderlands' discourse. They present them as both specifically nostalgic and distinctly Central European.[17]

Inga Iwasiów's novel is set in the Western Pomeranian city of Szczecin. It covers the years 1957 to 1981, but also includes references to the 1930s and 1940s. One of Iwasiów's protagonists, Marysia, is born in a village between Drohobycz and Sambor in today's Ukraine. She comes to Szczecin after her family's relocation to Silesia. Joanna Bator's text, on the other hand, is set predominantly in the time between the 1960s and 1989, also including references to pre-war life and additionally foreshadowing a post-socialist future. It is mainly set in Wałbrzych, a Lower Silesian coal miners' town, where Władek and Halina Chmura are forcibly resettled from a village close to Grodno in today's Belarus. Their granddaughter Dominika is the main character of the novel.

---

[16] For the controversy on the terminology, the inherent nostalgia and the role of the discourse in literature, cf. Bogusław Bakuła, "Colonial and Postcolonial Aspects of Polish Borderlands Studies: An Outline," Trans. by Tadeusz Z. Wolanski and Anna Warso. *Teksty Drugie* 1 (2014): 96–123. Following Bakuła's argument, I will use the term in inverted commas as it is symbolic of a colonialist appropriation of the region by the Polish, cf. ibid., 99.

[17] Connections between the two novels have been made before, cf. Ursula Phillips, "Problems of Feminism and Postfeminism in Novels by Inga Iwasiów and Joanna Bator," in *Women's voices and feminism in Polish cultural memory,* ed. Urszula Chowaniec and Ursula Phillips (Newcastle upon Tyne: Cambridge Scholars 2012), 127–154.

It is significant that there is no substantial difference in the novels between imagining a Ukrainian and a Belorussian variant of the 'Borderland' discourse. Instead, both reduce the idea of a specific space to vague and mythologized far-away lands. Yet in their unclear national affiliation and historicity, the so-installed 'Borderlands' join the league of typically Central European regions. It is important to note that it is not an independent heterodiegetic narrator who presents the image of the 'Borderlands', but rather the characters themselves, namely Marysia and Władek, both of whom are prototypical nostalgics. How, then, are the 'Borderlands' configured as screens for projection, how can they be seen as chronotopes and how are they used to discard the present and criticize the system in place?

In *Bambino*, Marysia's emotional relationship with her origin is ambivalent. In the beginning of the novel, she rejects her descent because it makes her feel foreign in Szczecin. She is perceived by the others as different from them, especially due to her language and her inability to read the Latin alphabet. Her in-laws also dismiss her for not being Polish, because she was not born within the borders they understand to constitute Poland. In order to be accepted, she tries to break loose from her childhood in what is now the Ukrainian Soviet Republic. Together with her husband Janek, she decides that '[t]he past can go to hell!'[18]

However, she never entirely gives up on her memories. She feels warmly for the language she grew up with.[19] When she takes her daughter on a journey to her birthplace in 1972, she implicitly acknowledges the role of the 'Borderlands' in her life when she admits to still being in search of a 'different place to call home'.[20] She has not given up on her birthplace as her home just yet. The idea of a place where she feels rooted is projected onto the 'Borderlands', even though her arrival in Szczecin was already 15 years ago. As the present clashes with her memories of her home village, the narrator comments:

---

[18] Inga Iwasiów, *Bambino* (Warszawa: Świat Książki 2008), 97.
[19] Ibid., 238: "That borderland Polish, admittedly the most beautiful."
[20] Ibid., 257.

No, it is not that she remembers something completely different. She is not blinded with sentiment. No, she remembers it exactly like this. The creek close to the house, this year it is dried up. The houses, mainly wooden ones. The well grown, but fairly messy gardens. The outside privy. The orchard, not the best apples. Old trees. Across the picture she carries in her head, something like patina. A noble kind of decay, of coat. It is like that, but worse. Poorer, dirtier.[21]

Marysia herself, however, claims to be devoid of sentiment, but does acknowledge the patina that has thus covered her memories. Notions of the 'Borderlands' are expressed in a metaphor of a deteriorating object, something that has possibly even gained beauty in its romanticized decay. At the same time, they are presented as something symbolic of yet another life and, more importantly, another time. In the description of the underdevelopment, the idyllic stereotype of a simpler time shines through. Marysia's memories are dust-covered images that arise in the confrontation between her memories and the present, thus shifting the meaning of the moment entirely to the past. They are the semidarkness that Stasiuk proposes to symbolize Central Europe.

The images of the 'Borderlands' that Marysia presents are not only projections onto a space that has become unobtainable for her, but also thickly charged with a past that no longer exists. While Marysia understands that almost nothing has changed and the prototypical Central European village she comes back to poses an example for a nostalgic continuity, she is also confronted with the differences that can only be expressed by comparing the present with the past. There is a lack in the present that is voiced clearly—the village is now neither as wealthy nor as clean as it used to be. This is the reason why Marysia indulges even more in her nostalgic memories of her home in the aftermath of her visit.

Once Marysia's marriage with Janek has failed, she retreats to memory entirely.[22] A second visit to Ukraine is equally as disappointing as the first, but results in her understanding 'that, and this knowledge comes to her as a surprise, she had a real life there and would like to still be there.'[23] She

---

[21] Ibid., 262–263.
[22] Ibid., p. 341: "Marysia lives through remembering."
[23] Ibid., 342.

longs for an empty space she can project her childhood images onto. It is the space that grants her an identity that the present in Szczecin has denied her, for even in Janek's eyes she becomes a *ruska*, a 'Russian' , again as soon as they split up. Her nostalgia for the 'Borderlands' is a way of escaping the present whose deficiencies become ever so visible through her sufferings and finally culminate in her suicide.

In *Sand Mountain*, Władek's death is similarly set in scene as a result of his insatiable longing for his lost 'Borderland' home. He has cancer, but the defining characteristic of his existence is nostalgia. Consequently, his physical and his psychological sufferings morph into one: 'Władek Chmura was poisoned by longing (which he knew about) and a beginning illness (which he did not want to know about) [...].'[24] In the end, it is almost impossible to tell if he died from cancer or from a figuratively broken heart.

After his resettlement to Wałbrzych, Władek lives entirely on comparisons with his 'Borderland' past. He discredits everything in his present from the bread that used to taste better to the tools that used to work better. He puts his 'here' in perspective by aid of a mythologized, yet fairly undefined 'there':

> Sawdust, not bread, he said to Halina, there we had bread that a man could just eat and it tasted good, even when you just sprinkled a bit of salt on it. Sometimes, he remembered, I cut it when it was still warm and I could have half a loaf simply with salt, but the one here is just like clay. To Władek, everything was better there and when sometimes he was missing a good hammer to drive in a nail or boots for the winter, he said: there I had a hammer, or: there I had boots; and he never added anything to that, no specifics, because it was natural to him that the difference between the hammers and boots there and here was clear as the sun to everyone.[25]

There is no intrinsic need for Władek to specify any of his remarks on the yearned-for 'there'—he creates yet another empty space in the sense of Stasiuk that allows for projections of a better, brighter life. For the reader, the image of the 'Borderlands' remains to be a textual gap, because a recipient can have no knowledge of the space which Władek conjures up.

---

[24] Bator: *Piaskowa Góra*, 75.
[25] Bator, *Piaskowa Góra*, 76–77.

The vagueness of his descriptions allows for a deeply nostalgic impetus. At the same time, Władek's entire existence is a criticism of the deficient present.

The inability to get to the 'Borderlands' again enhances this, and in it lies also the temporal quality of the space. 'There' only exists in Władek's memories, it is frozen in time at the moment that he had to leave it. It is, therefore, largely configured through the historic moment in which it has stopped to develop in Władek's eyes. To him, the 'Borderlands' are still part of Poland, unlike for Marysia, who has to accept her own 'Borderlands' new affiliation with Soviet Ukraine.

Władek's suspicions of everything that is not from 'there' accelerates his death, as he even shies away from the local doctors, who he does not trust in curing him. His passing is then staged as a homecoming to the longed-for land:

> [...] shortly after he was walking through the meadow of his childhood, the last path he saw. His other hand, soft like a child's again, lay in his long deceased mother's palm, with her slanting eyes and swarthy skin which she had inherited on a genetic whim, who knows where from, maybe from a great great grandmother who had been raped by a soldier of Genghis Khan, he kept walking so long, until the meadow flashed up in a sudden explosion of light.[26]

Only in death can the temporal gap between the past and the present be filled and the pain be resolved. Notably, this cathartic moment is modelled in a landscape. Also, while Marysia has to endure changes to her 'Borderlands' and fails to accommodate her descent as a generator of identity, Władek in death returns to the exact place that he has perpetuated in a projection of the past. He does so, quite literally, nostalgically, as we know that nostalgia means an ache to return.

The 'Borderlands' configurations in both novels pose spaces that are objects to projection, defined by their past and used to criticize the present. The interpenetration of Central European and nostalgic notions is illustrated in this motif. Furthermore, for both Marysia and Władek, their past and their identity are ultimately the same thing, and nostalgic longings for

---

[26] Bator, *Piaskowa Góra*, 84.

their past are an expression of a perceived loss of self. At the same time, their own identity is perpetuated in the longing for the empty space that is Central Europe—that exact screen for projection, defined by the past and distancing itself from the experience of the present.

Milan Kundera has named Central Europe to be a 'fate.'[27] In that respect, the notion is capable of overcoming concepts of identity that are dependent on, for example, blood lineage, nationality, ethnicity or descent. Central Europe certainly supplies moments of identification that are able to deconstruct borders on maps and in minds. Its saturation with nostalgic potential does not have to hinder this. In fact, within this discourse on Central Europe, nostalgia can help to remind us of the common experiences and memories that Milan Kundera has evoked above. If Central Europe is the longing for the empty space that can be filled, and if what that is has not yet been finally decided, then the opportunity to create something substantial has not yet passed.

---

[27] Kundera: *Tragedy*, p. 35.

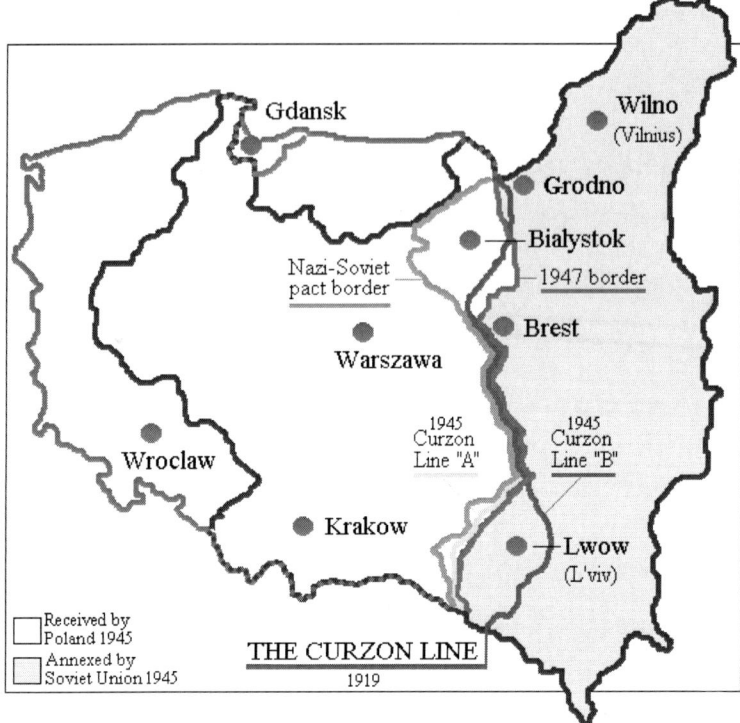

Figure 19: Postwar borders of Poland. Public Domain.

Abstract

In this essay, Andrzej Stasiuk's text *Dziennik* is used to draw parallels between his notion of Central Europe and the concept of nostalgia. It is conceived that both an imagined Central Europe and a nostalgically imagined past (1) function as projective screens, (2) intertwine space and time, and (3) dissociate themselves from the present as an ideologically charged reference frame. These structural similarities are exploited within a discussion of contemporary Polish literature, namely Inga Iwasiów's *Bambino* and Joanna Bator's *Sand Mountain*. Specifically, the 'Borderlands' discourse in these novels is shown to connect Central Europe, nostalgia, and prevailing questions of identity.

Keywords: nostalgia, Central Europe, Andrzej Stasiuk, Inga Iwasiów, Joanna Bator, borderlands, identity, Polish literature

Bibliography

Andrukhovych, Yurii. *Dezorijentacija na miscevosti. Sproby.* Ivano-Frankivsk: Lileja-NV 2006.

Bakhtin, Mikhail M.. *The Dialogic Imagination: Four Essays.* Translated by Caryl Emerson and Michael Holquist. Austin: University of Texas Press 1994.

Bakuła, Bogusław, "Colonial and Postcolonial Aspects of Polish Borderlands Studies: An Outline." Translated by Tadeusz Z. Wolanski and Anna Warso. *Teksty Drugie* 1 (2014): 96–123.

Bator, Joanna. *Piaskowa Góra.* Warszawa: W.A.B. 2009.

Hofer, Johannes, "Medical Dissertation on Nostalgia by Johannes Hofer, 1688." Translated by Carolyn Kiser Anspach. *Bulletin of the Institute of the History of Medicine* 2 (1934): 376–391.

Howard, Scott Alexander, „Nostalgia," *Analysis* 72, no 4 (2012): 641–650.

Iwasiów, Inga. *Bambino.* Warszawa: Świat Książki 2008.

Kliems, Alfrun, "Aggressiver Lokalismus: Undergroundästhetik, Antiurbanismus und Regionsbehauptung bei Andrzej Stasiuk und Jurij Andruchovyč." *Zeitschrift für Slawistik* 56, 2 (2011): 197–213.

Kundera, Milan, "The Tragedy of Central Europe." Translated by Edmund White. *New York Review of Books*, 26.04.1984: 33–38.

Milosz, Czeslaw. *Native Realm. A search for self-definition.* Translated by Catherine S. Leach. Berkeley: University of California Press 1981.

Naumann, Friedrich. *Mitteleuropa.* Berlin: Reimer 1915.

Phillips, Ursula, "Problems of Feminism and Postfeminism in Novels by Inga Iwasiów and Joanna Bator," in *Women's voices and feminism in Polish cultural memory,* ed. Urszula Chowaniec and Ursula Phillips. Newcastle upon Tyne: Cambridge Scholars 2012, 127–154.

Rüb, Matthias, "Wo liegt Mitteleuropa?" *Kafka – Zeitschrift für Mitteleuropa* 1, 1 (2001): 14–21.

Schlögel, Karl, "Die Mitte liegt ostwärts. Die Deutschen, der verlorene Osten und Mitteleuropa." in *Die Mitte liegt ostwärts. Europa im Übergang,* Karl Schlögel. Frankfurt am Main: Fischer 2008, 14–64.

Stasiuk, Andrzej, "Dziennik Okrętowy." in *Moja Europa. Dwa eseje o Europie zwanej Środkową,* ed. Jurij Andruchowycz and Andrzej Stasiuk. Wołowiec: Czarne 2001, 75–140.

Stasiuk, Andrzej. *Tales of Galicia.* Translated by Margarita Nafpaktitis. Prague: Twisted Spoon Press 2003.

Stasiuk, Andrzej. *Dukla.* Translated by Bill Johnston. Champaign, Dublin et al.: Dalkey Archive Press 2011.

Stasiuk, Andrzej. *On the Road to Babadag. Travels in the other Europe,* Translated by Michael Kandel. Boston, New York: Houghton Mifflin Harcourt 2011.

Tellkamp, Uwe. *Der Turm.* Frankfurt am Main: Suhrkamp 2008.

Starobinski, Jean, "The Idea of Nostalgia." *Diogenes* 14 (1966): 81–103

AUTHOR INFORMATION

Magdalena Baran-Szołtys is a Ph.D. candidate at the Doctoral Program 'Austrian Galicia and its Multicultural Heritage' and research associate at the research cluster 'Mobile Cultures and Societies' at the University of Vienna. She holds an M.A. in Germanic Studies and an M.A. in Slavic Studies, both from the University of Vienna. She was a tutor in German Language and Literature at the University of Sydney and a visiting scholar at the Institute of Polish Studies at the Jagiellonian University, University of Wrocław, and at the Ukrainian Research Institute at Harvard University. Co-organizer of the international conference *Galicia in Motion* (in cooperation with the Wien Museum and Polish Academy of Sciences, 2015). Co-editor of the book *Galizien in Bewegung. Wahrnehmungen – Begegnungen – Verflechtungen* (Göttingen: Vienna University Press at V&R unipress 2018), as well as of the special issue *The Central European Archaeology of Knowledge: Exploring Polish and Ukrainian Literature (1989–2014)* of the journal *Central Europe* (vol. 15/1–2, 2017).

Monika Glosowitz is a research and teaching assistant at the University of Silesia. She holds PhDs from the University of Silesia and the University of Oviedo. She graduated from the Interdepartmental Individual Studies in Humanities of the University of Silesia and also holds M.A. degrees from Utrecht University and the University of Granada. She works as an associated editor of the journals *artPapier*, *Opcje*, and *Polish-Canadian Comparative Studies*. Co-editor of the book *Discourses of Hospitality* (Warszawa 2018) and of the special issue *The Central European Archeology of Knowledge: Exploring Polish and Ukrainian Literature (1989–2014)* of the journal *Central Europe* (2017, vol. 15), as well as of the special issue *Hospitality* of the journal *Opcje* (2016, vol. 3). She has published on Polish contemporary literature and affective theories and translated excerpts from Michel Foucault's, Rosi Braidotti's, Sara Ahmed's and Luce Irigaray's work into Polish.

Mariella C. Gronenthal holds a B.A. in German Studies and Polish Studies from the University of Greifswald, an M.A. and a PhD in Comparative Literature from the University of Tübingen (*Nostalgia and Socialism— Emotional Memory in German and Polish Contemporary Literature*, 2018). She was a research assistant at the Slavonics Department at Humboldt University of Berlin from 2011 until the completion of her doctoral dissertation in 2016. Since then she has been working as a human rights educator, focusing on intercultural exchange. Her research interests include nostalgia and memory studies, transculturality, theories of fiction and the intermedial play of literature and music.

Aleksandra Konarzewska successfully defended her Ph.D. dissertation at the Institute of Slavic Languages and Literatures at the University of Tübingen. She studied philosophy, history, religious studies, and Slavic literature at the University of Warsaw, Jagiellonian University in Cracow, Free University Berlin, and Yale University. At Yale, she used to work as a tutor in Eastern European History and Intellectual History. Co-editor of the special issue *The Central European Archeology of Knowledge: Exploring Polish and Ukrainian Literature (1989–2014)* of the journal *Central Europe* (2017, vol. 15).

Iris Llop holds a B.A. in Literary Studies from the University of Barcelona (Spain) and an M.A. in Literary Theory and Comparative Literature from the University of Barcelona (Spain). She is currently a PhD student and FPU Fellow in the Hispanic Philology, Literary Theory and Communication department at the University of Barcelona. Her research interests include the study of the concepts of 'thinking novel' and 'novelistic meditation' developed by Milan Kundera in his literary essays and the analysis of different forms of narrative reflection in the European modernist novel.

Jagoda Wierzejska is a historian of contemporary literature and culture, an adjunct professor in the Department of Literature of the 20th and 21st century at the Faculty of Polish Studies, University of Warsaw (Poland). In 2011 she defended her PhD and won the Prize of the Archives of Polish Emigration for the best PhD dissertation on the emigration topic. A member of the editorial board of the journal *Przegląd Humanistyczny* [*The Humanistic Review*]. The author of the book *Retoryczna interpretacja autobiograficzna. Na przykładzie pisarstwa Andrzeja Bobkowskiego, Zygmunta Haupta i Leo Lipskiego* [*Rhetorical interpretation of the autobiography. The cases of writing of Andrzej Bobkowski, Zygmunt Haupt and Leo Lipski*] (2012). The co-author of the international project *Galician Polyphony. Places and Voices* (2014–2015). A fellow of the Center for Urban History of East Central Europe, Lviv (2016) and the University of Vienna (2017).

ILLUSTRATIONS

Figure 1: *Revue du Pays de Caux. Le chaos Austro-hongrois en 1900*; Date: 1902; Author: Pierre de Coubertin; source: Bibliothèque nationale de France; URL: https://commons.wikimedia.org/wiki/File:Revue_du_Pays_de_Caux_n1_mars_1902_(page_31_crop).jpg. Public Domain.

Figure 2: *Triangle of three emperors, Mysłowice/Sosnowiec (Poland). Three emperors from the left: Nicholas II of Russia, Wilhelm II of Prussia, Franz Joseph I of Austria*; Date: between 1907 and 1917; Author: [unknown]; Source: Scan from the old post card; URL: https://commons.wikimedia.org/wiki/File:Tr_3_cesarzy_20005.JPG. Public Domain.

Figure 3: *"Europa Zukunftstkarte" Albert Rymann*; Date: [no data]; Author: Albert Rymann [Alban Rumann]; Source: "Ilustrowany Kuryer Codzienny" nr 213, 4 sierpnia 1939, s. 2, art. "Przyszła mapa Europy"; URL: https://commons.wikimedia.org/wiki/File:Europa_Zukunfstkarte_Albert_Rymann.JPG. Public Domain.

Figure 4: *Europe before and after the WWI*; Date: [1924?]; Source: Carnegie Endowment for Peace 1924; URL: https://commons.wikimedia.org/wiki/File:Europe_1914_and_1924.png. Public Domain.

Figure 5: *Interior of the Holy Trinity Chapel in Lublin*; Date: 2017; Author: Artinpl; URL: https://commons.wikimedia.org/wiki/File:Interior_of_the_Holy_Trinity_Chapel_in_Lublin_10.jpg. Creative Commons CC0 1.0 Universal Public Domain Dedication (https://creativecommons.org/publicdomain/zero/1.0/deed.en).

Figure 6: *Беларуская (тарашкевіца): Берасьце (Bieraście), праспэкт Бульварны (praspekt Bulvarny)*; Date: Sept 22, 1939; Author: [unknown]; URL: https://be-tarask.wikipedia.org/wiki/Файл:Bieraście,_Bulvarny._Берасьце,_Бульварны_(22.09.1939).jpg. Public Domain.

Figure 7: *Podpisanie porozumień sierpniowych w Gdańsku, w sali BHP - mural w Gdańsku, na wiadukcie ul. Okopowej. Osoby w pierwszym rzędzie od lewej: 3-ci Mieczysław Jagielski, 4-ty Lech Wałęsa, 5-ty Tadeusz Fiszbach*; Date: March 24, 2011; Author: Artur Andrzej; URL: https://commons.wikimedia.org/wiki/File:Podpisanie_poroz umie%C5%84_sierpniowych_w_Gda%C5%84sku_-_graffiti_w_ Gda%C5%84sku.jpg. Public Domain.

Figure 8: *Zdjęcie uzyskane od www.kampania.org.pl i umieszczone za zgodą R. Biedronia na licencji PD*; Date: Feb 22, 2006 (original upload date); Author: Robert Biedroń; URL: https://commons.wiki media.org/wiki/File:Lesbijki.jpg. Creative Commons CC0 1.0 Universal Public Domain Dedication (https://creativecom mons.org/publicdomain/zero/1.0/deed.en).

Figure 9: *During the Soviet invasion of Czechoslovakia, Czechoslovaks carry their national flag past a burning tank in Prague. Photo from "CIA Analysis of the Warsaw Pact Forces: The Importance of Clandestine Reporting" For more information, visit the CIA's Historical Collections page (www.cia.gov/library/publications/histo rical-collection-pu...)*; Date: 1968; Author: The Central Intelligence Agency; URL: https://commons.wikimedia.org/wiki/File:10 _Soviet_Invasion_of_Czechoslovakia_-_Flickr_-The_Central_In telligence_Agency.jpg. Public Domain.

Figure 10: *Diet of Galicia and Lodomeria in Lwov, constructed during the Austro-Hungarian reign. After World War I it was turned into the building of Lviv University*; Date: before 1898; Author: Edward Trzemeski; Source: Julius Laurencic (Hrsg.): *Unsere Monarchie – Die österreichischen Kronländer zur Zeit des fünfzigjährigen Regierungs-Jubiläums seiner k.u.k. apostol. Majestät Franz Joseph I.*, Georg Szelinski k.k. Universitäts-Buchhandlung, Wien 1898; URL: https://commons.wikimedia.org/wiki/File:Diet_of_Galicia_ and_Lodomeria.png. Public Domain.

Figure 11: *Jewish musicians (Faust family) from Rohatyn (modern western Ukraine). Klezmorim (Klezmers)—traditional musicians among Jews, most of them members of the Faust family. Rohatyn, 1912 (then in Galicia, Austro-Hungarian monarchy). Jewish klezmer music band, antique photo*; Date: 1912; Author: Unknown photographer from Rohatyn; Source: Jews in prewar Poland: http://my.opera.com/Cz%C4%99stochowa%20Moje%20Miasto/albums/showpic.dml?album=444845&picture=6200135; URL: https://commons.wikimedia.org/wiki/File:January_Suchodolski_-_Mohort_1859.jpg. Public Domain.

Figure 12: *Kaiser Karl I. besucht Czernowitz am 6. August*; Date: between 1915 and 1917; Author: unknown; URL: https://commons.wikimedia.org/wiki/File:01917_Kaiser_Karl_I._besucht_Czernowitz_am_6._August.jpg. Public Domain.

Figure 13: *Mohort*; Date: 1859; Author: January Suchodolski; URL: https://commons.wikimedia.org/wiki/File:January_Suchodolski_-_Mohort_1859.jpg. Public Domain.

Figure 14: *Ukrainian Lemkos (Carpathian highlanders) from south east Poland. Old prewar photo*; Date: [before 1939?]; Author: [no data]; Source: NAC digital archives – http://audiovis.nac.gov.pl/haslo/102:310/. URL: https://pl.wikipedia.org/wiki/Plik:Ukrainian_Lemkos_-_Lemky.jpg. Public Domain.

Figure 15: *Wołowiec, Cerkiew Opieki Matki Bożej w Wołowcu*; Date: Aug 21 2017, Author: Harcik; URL: https://commons.wikimedia.org/wiki/File:Cerkiew_Wo%C5%82owiec.jpg. Creative Commons Attribution 3.0 Unported license (https://creativecommons.org/licenses/by/3.0/deed.en).

Figure 16: *Tomb effigy of Amalia Mniszech (1736-1772)*; Date: 1773; Author: Jan Obrocki; Photographer: Mathiasrex Maciej Szczepańczyk (2009); URL: https://commons.wikimedia.org/wiki/File:Tomb_effigy_of_Amalia_Mniszech_in_Saint_Mary_Magdalene_Church_in_Dukla.JPG. Creative Commons Attribution 3.0 Unported license (https://creativecommons.org/licenses/by/3.0/deed.en).

Figure 17: *Deutsch: Leute aus Oberschlesien um 1932*; Author: Leon Malhomme; Source: Digital Library of Silesian Voivodeship (www.sbc.org.pl); Date: 1932; URL: https://commons.wikimedia.org/wiki/File:Leute_aus_Oberschlesien_1.jpg. Public Domain.

Figure 18: *Deutsch: Zelasno (1934-1945 Eisenau)*; Date: 1939; Author: unknown; Source: http://dolny-slask.org.pl/5662105,foto.html?idEntity=539427; URL: https://commons.wikimedia.org/wiki/File:%C5%BBelazna_Zelasno_Eisenau_Oberschlesien_.jpg. Public Domain.

Figure 19: *Map of Poland in 1945*; Date: Dec 2, 2005; Author: Adam Carr; URL: https://en.wikipedia.org/wiki/File:Map_of_Poland_(1945).png. Public Domain.

INDEX OF NAMES

A

Alexievich, Svietlana A. 100
Amar, Tarik Cyril 63, 79
Andrukhovych, Sofia 76, 77
Andrukhovych, Yurii (Andruchovyč, Jurij / Andruchowycz, Jurij / Andruchowytsch, Juri) 21, 23, 70, 75, 83, 87, 98, 99, 100, 102, 103, 105, 106, 115, 121, 122, 123, 125, 126, 127, 128, 131, 133, 145, 146
Anjou, Jadwiga (Jadwiga of Anjou / Jadwiga of Poland) 15, 24
Anspach, Carolyn Kiser 135, 145
Árpád, Coloman (Coloman, King of Halych and Duke of Slavonia / Coloman of Galicia / Koloman / Kálmán) 55
Augé, Marc 116

B

Bakhtin, Mikhail M. 40, 135, 145
Bakuła, Bogusław 93, 94, 121, 122, 138, 145
Baran-Szołtys, Magdalena 5, 87, 92, 111, 115, 122, 126, 147
Barta, Peter I. 11, 23, 24
Batlle, Carles (Batlle i Jordà, Carles) 116, 127
Bator, Joanna 134, 138, 141, 142, 144, 145
Bauman, Zygmunt 11, 23
Beethoven, Ludvig van 29
Behr, August 59
Berger, Tilman 7
Berwanger, Katrin 113, 124
Bialasiewicz, Luiza 66, 70, 79

Bianchini, Stefano 38, 47
Bilewicz, Aleksandra 94, 125
Blobaum, Robert 62, 80
Bobrzyński, Michał 65
Bömelburg, Hans-Jürgen 94, 122
Borkowska, Grażyna 94, 122
Boyer-Weinmann, Martine 28, 47, 48
Boym, Svetlana 111, 112, 122
Brandys, Kazimierz 67, 79
Bretschneir, Heinrich Gottfried 59
Broch, Hermann 34, 37, 41, 43
Brodsky, Joseph 11, 23
Bunin, Ivan A. 31
Burzyńska-Kamienicka, Anna 94, 123, 127
Buszko, Józef, 65, 79
Büttner, Ruth 102, 126

C

Chowaniec, Urszula 138, 145
Chvatik, Kvetoslav 42, 47
Cytacka, Agnieszka 96, 122
Czaplińska, Maria 110, 122
Czuma, Mieczysław 72, 80

D

Dabrowski, Patrice 7
Dimitrova, Blaga 40, 47
Długosz, Magdalena 97, 123
Domínguez, César 44
Donskis, Leonidas 28, 38, 43, 47, 48
Dostoyevsky, Fyodor M. 11, 23, 31
Drews-Sylla, Gesine 7
Drozda, Thomas 99
Dubasevych, Roman 97, 122
Dunn, James 7

E

Emerson, Caryl 135, 145

F

Faber, Martin 41, 47, 97, 123
Fedyuk, Olena, 72, 73, 80
Finkielkraut, Alain 34, 35, 47
Fiut, Aleksander 70, 80
Frank, Susi K. 102
Franzos, Karl Emil 59, 61, 62, 80, 84
Fras, Zbigniew 72, 80
Freud, Sigmund (Freud, Sigmund Shlomo) 37

G

Gáfrik, Róbert 105, 128
Garton Ash, Timothy 10, 17, 23
Glosowitz, Monika 147
Gnauck, Gerhard 100, 123
Goethe, Johann Wolfgang von 44
Gogol, Nikolai V. 31
Golec, Janusz 93, 123
Golemo, Karolina 93, 128
Gombrowicz, Witold 41
Gosk, Hanna 94, 123
Greig, David 116, 127
Grenier, Yvon 40, 42, 47
Grodziski, Stanisław 55, 64, 72, 80
Gronenthal, Marielle 5, 131, 148
Groys, Boris 120, 123

H

Habsburg, Franz Joseph (Franz Joseph I, Emperor of Austria and King of Hungary / Franz Joseph I of Austria / Franz Josef I) 12, 13, 64, 68, 71, 151, 152
Habsburg, Maria Theresa (Maria Theresa, Archduchess of Austria and Queen of Bohemia and Hungary / Maria Theresia) 54, 57
Habsburg-Lorraine, Joseph (Joseph II, Holy Roman Emperor, King of Bohemia and Hungary / Joseph II / Josef II) 54, 56, 57, 60
Haen, Theo D. 44
Hafftka, Aleksander 69
Hagen, William W. 62, 80
Haid, Elisabeth 90, 123
Halecki, Oskar 15, 23, 24
Hamšík, Dušan 29, 47
Hann, Christopher 51, 79, 81, 82
Hanus, Anna 102, 126
Hašek, Jaroslav 38, 41
Havel, Václav 17, 24, 29, 48, 49
Heffernan, Michael 64, 80
Henning Hahn, Hans 93, 124
Herbert, Zbigniew 99
Hibel, Katarzyna 66, 80
Hnatiuk, Ola 72, 81
Hobsbawm, Eric 74, 81
Hofer, Johannes 134, 135, 145
Holquist, Michael 135, 145
Horel, Catherine 11, 24
Horstmann, Jakob 7
Howard, Scott Alexander 145
Hrytsak, Yaroslav 73, 81
Hubert, Stanisław 55, 81
Hundorova, Tamara 7, 76, 82
Hutcheon, Linda 68, 81

I

Iłłakowicz, Krystyna 7
Ishov, Zakhar 7
Ivanova, Velichka 40, 47
Iwasiów, Inga 138, 139, 144, 145

J

Jabłoński, Dariusz 116
Jagodzinski, Sabine 96, 97, 123
Janáček, Leoš (Janáček, Leo Eugen) 38
Janicka, Anna 93, 124
Janion, Maria 95, 96, 123
Johnston, Bill 115, 123, 146
Judt, Tony 10, 11, 24
Jung, Carl Gustav 37

… Index of Names

K

Kadłubek, Zbigniew 7
Kafka, Franz 33, 34, 37, 41, 131, 145
Kałążny, Jerzy 95, 127
Kalinka, Walerian 65
Kandel, Michael 70, 83, 146
Karpa, Irena 100
Khan, Genghis 142
Kieniewicz, Stefan 65, 81, 94, 123
Kiš, Danilo 32, 100
Kłańska, Maria 57, 81
Kliems, Alfrun 103, 123, 133, 145
Klimt, Gustav 76
Kolbuszewski, Jacek 93, 94, 95, 123
Kołodziejczyk, Dorota 94, 124
Kolpak, Karolina 7
Konarzewska, Aleksandra 5, 9, 148
Koper, Sławomir 94, 124
Kortum, Ernst Bogumil 59
Kos, Wolfgang 54, 83, 93, 113, 125
Kosta, Peter 113, 124
Kostyrko, Vlodko (Kostyrko, Volodymyr) 74, 75, 81
Kowal, Grzegorz 93, 124
Kowalczyk, Jerzy 110, 124
Kowalski, Grzegorz 93, 124
Kozłowski, Maciej 62, 63, 81
Kożuchowski, Adam 93, 124
Kratter, Franz 58, 59, 61, 81
Kundera, Milan 5, 9, 11, 12, 22, 23, 24, 27, 28, 29, 30, 31, 32, 33, 34, 35, 36, 37, 38, 39, 40, 41, 42, 43, 44, 45, 46, 47, 48, 49, 69, 81, 89, 104, 105, 124, 131, 133, 135, 136, 143, 145, 148
Kuśniewicz, Andrzej 67, 68, 69, 82

L

Le Grand, Eva 42, 48
Leach, Catherine S. 69, 83, 145

Lem, Stanisław 99, 153
Lipiński, Krzysztof 91, 124
Llop, Iris 5, 27, 148
Łoyko, Felix 55

M

Maciejewski, Janusz 96, 124
Magocsi, Paul R. 51, 79, 81, 82
Magris, Claudio 48
Mahler, Gustav 37
Mandelstam, Osip E. 31
Maner, Hans-Christian 54, 83
Margelik, Johann Wenzel 60
Marszałek, Magdalena 89, 91, 96, 97, 100, 102, 104, 113, 122, 124, 125
Matějka Ladislav 29, 48
Matvejević, Predrag 12
May, Suzanne 7
Meller, Katarzyna 102, 124
Mellor, Jane 12
Mick, Christoph 63, 83
Miłosz, Czesław 32, 35, 69, 83
Miniger, Jay D. 43, 48
Misiak, Małgorzata 94, 123, 127
Misurella, Fred 28, 48
Mniszech, Jerzy August (Mniszech, Jerzy August Wandalin) 110
Mniszech, Maria Amalia (Maria Amalia Mniszchowa, née Brühl / Amelia Maria Mniszchowa, née Brühl) 107, 110, 111, 112, 122, 153
Molisak Alina 72, 84
Mrożek, Sławomir 99
Musil, Robert 33, 34, 37, 38, 41, 43

N

Narvselius, Eleonora 75, 83
Naumann, Friedrich 106, 125, 131, 145
Nell, Werner 93, 124
Nemcova Banerjee, Maria 28, 48
Neumann, Birgit 96, 127
Neumann, Iver B. 12

Niedźwiedź, Jakub 97, 125
Nowicka, Ewa 94, 125

O

O'Keeffe, Terrence 112, 125
O'Loughlin, John 70, 79
O'Branagáin, Finn 7
Olszewski, Michał 106, 107, 125
Orłowicz, Mieczysław 109, 125

P

Partsch, Joseph 106, 125
Pasternak, Boris L. 31
Pavlyshyn, Marko 76, 82
Paźniewski, Włodzimierz 69, 82
Pelz, Annegret 7
Petrosanyak, Halyna 76, 77, 82
Phillips, Ursula 138, 145
Pilch, Jerzy 21, 22, 24
Pireddu, Nicoletta 48
Pol, Wincenty 92, 93, 97, 125
Pollack, Martin 21
Porta, Nicolas 48
Prokhasko, Taras 76, 77, 82
Prusin, Alexander V. 62, 82
Pucherová, Dobrota 105, 128
Purchla, Jacek 54, 83, 93, 113, 125

R

Ranger Terence 74, 81
Reimer, Georg 10, 24, 106, 125, 131, 145
Rewakowicz, Maria 72, 84, 111, 127
Rexheuser, Rex 110, 124
Riabchuk, Mykola 73, 82
Rilke, Rainer Maria (Rilke, René Karl Wilhelm Johann Josef Maria) 76
Rinner, Fridrun 91, 124, 125
Rizek, Martin 29, 30, 33, 34, 48
Romanov, Nicholas A. (Nicholas II, Emperor and Autocrat of All Russia / Nicholas Holstein-Gottorp-Romanov / Nicholas II of Russia / Nikolai II Aleksandrovich) 12, 69, 151
Roth, Philip 33, 48
Różewicz, Tadeusz 99
Rüb, Matthias 131, 145
Röskau-Rydel, Isabel 57, 81

S

Sabatos, Charles 29, 48
Said, Edward 53, 102
Sasse, Sylvia 89, 102, 122, 125
Saturczak, Łukasz 71, 83
Schahadat, Schamma 7
Schimsheimer, Christof 92, 102, 126
Schiper, Ignacy 69, 83
Schlögel, Karl 104, 106, 115, 116, 126, 132, 146
Schmitt, Eric-Emmanuel 48
Schnür-Pepłowski, Stanisław 59, 83
Scholz, Piotr O. 97, 123
Schönberg, Arnold (Schoenberg, Arnold Franz Walter) 37
Schöpflin, George 10, 11, 12, 23, 24
Schultes, Joseph August 59
Schwarz, Egon 12
Shore, Marci 7
Sid, Igor' 102, 126
Šimečka, Milan 12
Simonek, Stefan 91, 128
Smit, Amelia 7
Smolka, Stanisław 65
Sniadanko, Natalka 100
Snyder, Timothy 7, 10, 21, 24
Spiridon, Olivia 7
Starobinski, Jean 135, 146
Stasiuk, Andrzej 5, 21, 23, 70, 83, 87, 88, 89, 90, 91, 96, 97, 98, 99, 100, 101, 102, 103, 104, 105, 106, 107, 108, 109, 110, 111, 112, 113, 114, 115, 116, 117, 118, 119, 120, 121, 122, 123, 124, 125, 126, 127, 128, 129, 131, 132, 133, 134, 135, 136, 140, 141, 144, 145, 146

Stefanowska, Lidia 72, 84, 111, 127
Steiner, Carl 62, 84
Stojowski, Andrzej 69, 84
Stößinger, Renate 94, 122
Stryjkowski Julian 68, 69, 84
Suleja, Włodzimierz 94, 127
Swieykowski, Emmanuel 109, 127
Syrnyk, Jarosław 94, 127
Szczerek, Ziemowit 21
Szczypiorski, Andrzej 99
Szujski, Józef 65

T

Tartakower, A. 69, 83
Tellkamp, Uwe 134, 146
Thirovin, Marie-Odile 28, 48
Thomsen, Mads Rosendahl 44
Todorova, Maria (Todorova, Marija N.) 11, 24
Topol, Jáchym 100
Tötösy de Zepetnek, Steven 49
Traunpaur, Alphons H. 58, 59, 84
Tropper, Elisabeth 116, 127
Trumpener, Kate 7
Trybuś, Krzysztof 95, 127

U

Uffelmann, Dirk 7, 96, 127
Ugrešić, Dubravka 11, 24, 25

V

Vajda, Mihàly 12
Veteranyi, Aglaja 100
Vozniak, Taras 74, 84
Vushko, Iryna 52, 84

W

Walder, Dennis 110, 127
Warso, Anna 138, 145

Wasiucionek, Michał 7
Wedemann, Marek 95, 127
Weismann, Stephanie 90, 123
Wereszycki, Henryk 55, 65, 84
Weretiuk, Oksana 102, 127
West, Tim 29
Wettin, Augustus Frederick (Augustus III Wettin, King of Poland, Grand Duke of Lithuania, Elector of Saxony / Augustus III of Poland / August III / Frederick Augustus II / Friedrich August II) 110
White, Edmund 69, 81, 124, 131, 145
White, Kenneth 101
Wiącek, Elżbieta 93, 128
Wiegandt, Ewa 66, 84, 113, 128
Wierzejska, Jagoda 5, 51, 63, 66, 71, 72, 84, 85, 89, 99, 105, 106, 128, 148
Wojciechowski, Piotr 68, 69, 85
Wojcieszuk, Krystian 7
Wojtyła, Karol (pope John Paul II, Ioannes Paulus II / Wojtyła, Karol Józef) 117
Wolanski, Tadeusz Z. 138, 145
Woldan, Alois 7, 66, 85, 91, 113, 128
Wolff, Larry (Wolff, Lawrence) 55, 56, 57, 60, 61, 62, 65, 66, 85, 90, 128
Wood, Nancy 10, 11, 23, 24
Woods, Michele 28, 49

Z

Zaleska Onyshkevych, Larissa M. L. 72, 84, 111, 127
Zayarnyuk, Andriy 55, 85
Zelenka, Milos 49
Zerboni di Sposetti, Wilhelm 59
Zerinschek, Klaus 91, 124, 125
Zhadan, Serhiy 100

INDEX OF SUBJECTS

1

1772 51, 52, 54, 55, 57, 58, 79, 81, 82, 85, 91, 109, 111, 154
1867 52, 65, 80, 85, 86
1918 51, 55, 57, 62, 63, 66, 81, 82, 86, 91, 94
1945 38, 58, 69, 70, 82, 94, 95, 129, 155
1956 36, 37, 67
1968 29, 31, 36, 37, 39, 48, 49, 69, 77, 85, 153
1980, 1980s 10, 11, 19, 22, 24, 28, 30, 33, 41, 46, 49, 73, 90, 94
1984 5, 9, 24, 27, 28, 34, 35, 38, 43, 46, 47, 48, 69, 82, 90, 126, 133, 146
1989 9, 10, 11, 23, 24, 70, 72, 88, 90, 91, 94, 95, 106, 113, 123, 124, 128, 129, 139, 148, 149
1990, 1990s 10, 17, 19, 23, 28, 36, 48, 58, 62, 73, 82, 84, 85, 89, 90, 97, 104, 108, 111, 113, 117, 122, 129

2

2014 5, 9, 23, 32, 48, 54, 66, 77, 80, 81, 83, 90, 94, 95, 123, 124, 128, 139, 146, 148, 149, 150

A

absolutism 56
art 15, 16, 28, 44, 45, 46, 75, 111, 152
Austria, Austrian 9, 13, 14, 21, 33, 51, 52, 53, 54, 55, 57, 58, 60, 61, 62, 63, 64, 65, 66, 67, 68, 69, 72, 76, 77, 78, 79, 85, 88, 89, 90, 91, 92, 100, 104, 109, 115, 123, 130, 148, 152
Austria-Hungary, Austria-Hungarian 13, 21, 91, 92, 104
autonomy 16, 42, 65, 66, 74

B

backwardness 11, 53, 56, 57, 59, 60, 62, 64, 79, 101
Belarus, Belarussian 16, 94, 139
Berlin 9, 10, 17, 23, 24, 58, 61, 66, 81, 82, 85, 90, 98, 103, 107, 117, 124, 125, 126, 127, 132, 146, 149
border 15, 21, 53, 96
borderlands 14, 146
Budapest 13, 17, 23, 36, 71, 105

C

capitalism, capitalist 9, 21, 101, 106, 116, 117, 118, 137
center 104, 106, 107, 111, 116, 136
chronotope, chronotopic 108, 136, 139
city 15, 42, 62, 76, 111, 117, 139
civilization 11, 14, 33, 36, 42, 53, 54, 56, 59, 60, 64, 65, 66, 75, 79, 118
Commonwealth, Polish-Lithuanian Commonwealth 51, 53, 54, 55, 57, 60, 65, 66, 67, 93, 94, 97
communism, communist 9, 16, 17, 19, 39
construction 29, 30, 34, 40, 44, 46, 47, 88, 92, 98, 106, 110, 123, 133
country 19, 29, 31, 32, 39, 40, 54, 55, 56, 74, 137

Cracow (Kraków, Krakau) 15, 54, 55, 57, 59, 62, 65, 68, 70, 71, 72, 80, 81, 82, 83, 84, 85, 90, 94, 96, 111, 125, 127, 128, 129, 130, 149

culture, cultural 9, 12, 13, 14, 15, 17, 19, 21, 32, 33, 34, 35, 36, 37, 38, 39, 40, 41, 42, 43, 44, 45, 46, 47, 53, 54, 60, 61, 62, 63, 64, 65, 66, 67, 72, 73, 74, 75, 76, 78, 79, 96, 97, 102, 103, 107, 108, 110, 117, 123, 131, 132, 133, 134, 135, 139, 146, 149

Czechia, Czech 9, 12, 15, 19, 21, 28, 29, 31, 32, 33, 34, 36, 38, 39, 40, 42, 43, 44, 45, 49

Czechoslovakia, Czechoslovak 10, 16, 17, 29, 31, 39, 153

D

Danube 51, 59, 62, 64, 65, 67, 71, 73, 78, 92

democracy 11, 35, 66, 71

discourse 12, 29, 30, 35, 40, 41, 64, 66, 70, 72, 73, 74, 85, 93, 94, 96, 99, 100, 101, 107, 122, 134, 139, 140, 144, 145

Dukla 89, 90, 108, 109, 110, 111, 112, 113, 114, 115, 116, 117, 119, 122, 123, 125, 128, 131, 135, 147, 154

E

East 5, 9, 11, 13, 15, 23, 24, 29, 32, 35, 36, 45, 49, 51, 52, 53, 60, 61, 62, 63, 65, 66, 68, 69, 71, 73, 76, 77, 78, 79, 83, 88, 89, 90, 92, 93, 96, 97, 98, 99, 100, 102, 103, 104, 105, 106, 108, 113, 115, 116, 118, 119, 120, 121, 122, 123, 136, 137, 150

Eastern 5, 11, 12, 13, 14, 15, 16, 17, 19, 24, 33, 36, 38, 40, 47, 48, 51, 53, 55, 56, 60, 61, 62, 63, 64, 66, 67, 68, 69, 70, 72, 73, 74, 75, 77, 78, 79, 80, 86, 90, 91, 96, 100, 101, 139, 149

Easterness 78, 79

East-West 9, 78, 90, 92, 104, 106, 120, 123

emptiness 88, 102, 120, 132

Enlightenment 53, 54, 56, 57, 60, 61, 65, 78, 79, 86, 100, 101

essay 9, 21, 27, 38, 41, 43, 44, 88, 89, 99, 105, 107, 132, 133, 134, 135, 145

Europe 9, 11, 12, 13, 14, 15, 16, 20, 21, 23, 24, 27, 28, 29, 30, 33, 34, 36, 37, 38, 40, 41, 42, 43, 44, 45, 47, 48, 49, 52, 53, 56, 60, 63, 64, 69, 70, 71, 72, 73, 74, 76, 77, 78, 79, 80, 81, 84, 85, 88, 90, 92, 97, 98, 99, 100, 101, 103, 104, 105, 106, 107, 113, 116, 117, 126, 129, 130, 132, 135, 136, 147, 152

Central Europe 5, 7, 9, 10, 11, 12, 13, 14, 15, 16, 17, 19, 21, 22, 23, 24, 27, 28, 29, 30, 32, 33, 34, 35, 37, 38, 40, 41, 42, 43, 45, 46, 47, 48, 49, 51, 55, 68, 69, 70, 71, 73, 74, 88, 89, 90, 99, 100, 104, 105, 106, 107, 109, 122, 123, 130, 132, 133, 134, 135, 136,137, 138, 139, 140, 141, 143, 144, 145, 146, 148, 149

East Central Europe 11, 15, 23, 24, 150

Eastern Europe 11, 12, 13, 16, 17, 19, 24, 33, 36, 38, 40, 48, 56, 61, 62, 86, 90, 100, 101, 149

Middle Europe 5, 9, 10, 88, 89, 90, 91, 92, 97, 98, 99, 101, 103, 104, 105, 106, 107, 108, 109, 116, 117, 118, 119, 120, 121, 122, 123

exile 32, 38, 39, 46, 47, 69, 136

experience 10, 21, 22, 31, 32, 35, 38, 39, 44, 45, 46, 60, 61, 144

F

figure 15, 111, 112, 116, 137
freedom 11, 65, 71, 75, 94
future 10, 11, 113, 114, 122, 139

G

Galicia (Galicja, Galizien) 5, 9, 22, 23, 51, 52, 53, 54, 55, 56, 57, 58, 59, 60, 61, 62, 63, 64, 65, 66, 67, 68, 69, 70, 71, 72, 73, 74, 75, 76, 77, 78, 79, 80, 81, 82, 83, 84, 85, 86, 90, 91, 92, 93, 94, 95, 96, 98, 99, 101, 103, 104, 106, 107, 109, 110, 111, 113, 114, 115, 116, 117, 121, 122, 123, 124, 125, 126, 127, 128, 130, 134, 135, 147, 148, 153, 154
    Austrian Galicia 52, 85, 88, 89, 90, 91, 109, 123, 148
    Galician identity 23, 68
geography 32, 53, 60, 62, 64, 66, 71, 78, 79, 88, 103, 108, 114, 121, 123, 132, 135
geopoetics 101, 102, 103, 123, 127, 130
Germany, German 7, 9, 10, 14, 15, 17, 19, 20, 21, 45, 52, 54, 56, 57, 59, 61, 62, 64, 88, 95, 105, 107, 132, 134, 136, 137, 139, 148, 149

H

Habsburg 13, 22, 51, 52, 55, 57, 58, 59, 60, 62, 64, 65, 66, 67, 68, 69, 70, 71, 73, 74, 75, 76, 77, 79, 86, 89, 91, 92, 104, 106, 109, 110, 111, 123, 130, 134
    Habsburg Empire 51, 65, 66, 69, 79, 89, 91, 109, 110, 111, 123

heritage 14, 15, 22, 46, 70, 73, 76, 91, 92, 98, 103, 104, 106, 108, 109, 111, 112, 115, 123
history 21, 33, 35, 36, 37, 39, 42, 44, 45, 46, 51, 60, 64, 65, 75, 76, 92, 95, 98, 103, 107, 108, 112, 116, 120, 121, 134, 135, 139, 149
Hungary, Hungarian 10, 12, 13, 15, 16, 19, 33, 36, 37, 55, 57, 65, 70, 72, 86, 97, 110, 134, 153, 154

I

identity 27, 28, 32, 33, 37, 38, 40, 42, 46, 47, 74, 93, 98, 122, 142, 143, 144, 145, 146
imagination 88, 110, 113, 115, 121, 132, 133
    imaginary 37, 68, 98, 103, 123
    imagined 12, 22, 23, 79, 103, 104, 110, 112, 116, 122, 123, 132, 138, 145
intellectual, intellectuals *(social group)* 10, 11, 27, 34, 42, 66, 73, 75, 76, 79, 94, 102, 108, 135
Iron Curtain 11, 23, 24, 36, 67, 94, 100
Ivano-Frankivsk (Stanislau, Stanisławów) 76, 77, 80, 83, 95, 117, 123, 146

J

Jews, Jewish 51, 53, 56, 59, 61, 62, 68, 83, 92, 109, 110, 111, 154
Josephinism, Josephinian 54, 55, 57, 60, 61, 62, 65, 78, 79, 86, 91, 130

K

Kresy 88, 91, 93, 94, 95, 96, 98, 103, 107, 123, 125, 128, 129
Kyiv 74, 77, 80, 83

L

land 51, 53, 57, 59, 60, 63, 65, 73, 76, 78, 79, 85, 94, 106, 110, 120, 121, 143
language 12, 13, 39, 42, 95, 140
Leipzig 58, 61, 81, 82, 85
life 28, 29, 37, 39, 42, 44, 58, 72, 91, 97, 103, 104, 112, 115, 117, 119, 139, 140, 141, 142
literature 9, 21, 27, 33, 37, 41, 43, 44, 46, 57, 58, 77, 79, 83, 88, 92, 94, 101, 117, 121, 135, 136, 139, 149
contemporary literature 148, 149
narrative 21, 23, 30, 38, 40, 42, 46, 47, 68, 93, 98, 110, 149
Polish literature 67, 71, 79, 101, 115, 123, 145, 146
prose 23, 32
travel literature (travel narratives) 21, 79, 90, 91, 123
Ukrainian literature 79
Lithuania, Lithuanian 14, 51, 53, 54, 55, 57, 60, 65, 66, 67, 93, 94, 97, 139
local 9, 12, 15, 16, 19, 21, 44, 55, 58, 72, 134, 143
Lviv (Lemberg, Lvov, Lwów) 52, 59, 62, 63, 71, 74, 75, 77, 80, 84, 110, 127, 150, 153

M

memory 39, 43, 46, 47, 91, 92, 93, 94, 95, 96, 105, 108, 111, 112, 113, 114, 115, 116, 134, 139, 141, 146, 149
metaphor 22, 95, 112, 135, 141
Mitteleuropa 10, 24, 48, 98, 107, 123, 125, 127, 132, 133, 137, 146, 147
moment 33, 111, 141, 143

N

nation 40, 44, 65, 75, 139
nobility 54, 59, 97, 114
non-place 116, 117, 118, 122, 123
nostalgia 21, 23, 40, 76, 98, 108, 112, 113, 114, 133, 134, 135, 136, 137, 138, 139, 142, 143, 144, 145, 146, 149
novel 11, 22, 29, 33, 36, 37, 38, 39, 40, 41, 42, 43, 44, 45, 46, 47, 67, 68, 69, 71, 77, 139, 140, 149

O

Orient 53, 54, 62, 84, 97, 103
orientalism 123
orientalization 97
Ostblock 11, 12

P

past 9, 11, 21, 22, 67, 73, 76, 98, 103, 104, 105, 109, 110, 112, 113, 114, 115, 117, 133, 134, 136, 137, 138, 139, 140, 141, 142, 143, 144, 145, 153
periphery 73, 91, 103, 104, 108
poetics 88, 89, 98, 99, 101, 105, 108, 114, 121
Poland, Polish 9, 10, 12, 15, 16, 17, 19, 21, 22, 25, 33, 36, 37, 51, 53, 54, 55, 57, 59, 60, 61, 62, 63, 64, 65, 66, 67, 68, 69, 70, 71, 72, 73, 78, 79, 80, 81, 85, 86, 88, 90, 91, 93, 94, 95, 96, 97, 98, 99, 100, 101, 110, 113, 114, 115, 117, 122, 123, 124, 127, 128,129, 130, 132, 134, 139, 140, 143, 145, 146, 148, 149, 152, 154, 155
politics, political 9, 16, 19, 24, 28, 30, 32, 34, 35, 37, 38, 39, 40, 41, 42, 44, 45, 46, 47, 51, 52, 54, 55, 60, 61, 63, 67, 70, 72, 78, 79, 88, 90, 97, 100, 101, 106, 107, 121, 133, 136, 137

post-socialist 102, 135, 136, 137, 139
Prague 13, 15, 17, 23, 31, 34, 36, 37, 39, 71, 90, 128, 147, 153
present 15, 22, 23, 30, 34, 46, 53, 64, 71, 91, 100, 103, 104, 112, 114, 115, 117, 119, 133, 134, 137, 138, 139, 140, 141, 142, 143, 144, 145
progress 11, 53, 60, 61, 102
projection 133, 134, 139, 140, 143, 144
province 51, 53, 54, 55, 56, 57, 58, 59, 60, 62, 63, 64, 65, 66, 67, 68, 69, 71, 72, 73, 75, 76, 78, 79, 91

R

Reformation 15, 33, 45
region 9, 10, 11, 16, 22, 23, 33, 35, 37, 52, 55, 56, 57, 58, 60, 61, 62, 63, 64, 66, 67, 72, 73, 74, 75, 76, 78, 79, 90, 91, 111, 116, 118, 120, 121, 135, 139
Renaissance 33, 45
resurrection 61, 112, 113, 118
rewriting 28, 47
Russia, Russian 9, 12, 13, 31, 33, 36, 37, 45, 51, 52, 53, 61, 62, 64, 65, 66, 67, 68, 69, 70, 74, 76, 77, 90, 100, 102, 103, 105, 134, 142, 152

S

Sarmatia, Sarmatian 88, 91, 97, 98, 103, 123
Silesia, Silesian 7, 9, 21, 133, 134, 138, 139, 148, 155
Slavic 7, 10, 15, 45, 54, 55, 62, 65, 86, 91, 93, 130, 148, 149
socialism, socialist 35, 76, 100, 106, 134, 136, 137
Soviet Union, Soviet 12, 13, 16, 17, 19, 20, 22, 31, 36, 38, 39, 63, 67, 74, 75, 76, 84, 102, 116, 136, 139, 140, 143, 153

space, spatial 9, 21, 22, 23, 37, 56, 68, 73, 74, 88, 89, 90, 91, 92, 95, 96, 98, 99, 102, 103, 104, 105, 107, 108, 109, 110, 111, 112, 113, 114, 115, 116, 117, 120, 121, 122, 123, 132, 133, 134, 135, 136, 137, 138, 140, 141, 142, 143, 144, 145
imagined space 22, 79, 123
spirituality 102, 113, 115, 118, 119
state 32, 37, 51, 54, 55, 56, 59, 60, 63, 65, 66, 76, 107, 112, 114

T

territory 38, 55, 60, 67, 75, 76, 77, 91, 95
text 21, 27, 32, 33, 36, 38, 44, 45, 55, 69, 107, 110, 111, 112, 113, 114, 115, 119, 121, 139, 145
time 7, 9, 15, 21, 31, 36, 42, 43, 45, 52, 53, 58, 60, 64, 66, 68, 75, 78, 79, 90, 97, 98, 99, 100, 105, 107, 108, 111, 112, 113, 114, 115, 117, 118, 119, 120, 121, 132, 133, 134, 135, 137, 138, 139, 141, 143, 144, 145
town 68, 110, 111, 114, 117, 119, 139
tradition 33, 34, 37, 38, 41, 42, 45, 46, 67, 70, 74, 75, 76, 77, 98, 134
tragedy 9, 24, 27, 34, 35, 36, 46, 48, 69, 82, 90, 106, 126, 132, 134, 136, 144, 146
transnational 91, 92, 98, 134
trauma 19
travel 21, 79, 90, 91, 94, 105, 110, 120, 123

U

Ukraine, Ukrainian 7, 9, 14, 16, 19, 21, 51, 53, 62, 63, 66, 67, 70, 71, 73, 74, 75, 76, 77, 78, 79, 80, 81, 83, 84, 85, 90, 94, 95, 99, 101, 113, 123, 129, 130,

134, 139, 140, 141, 143, 148, 149, 154

V

Vienna (Wien) 7, 13, 51, 53, 54, 58, 61, 66, 67, 68, 71, 72, 75, 76, 79, 81, 85, 86, 88, 93, 94, 113, 115, 117, 122, 123, 124, 125, 127, 128, 130, 148, 150, 153
village 101, 115, 117, 139, 140, 141

W

war 19, 33, 36, 42, 62, 66, 67, 139
   Cold War 9, 13, 32, 36, 38, 100, 136
   First World War 10
   Second World War 16
Warsaw 17, 23, 51, 64, 68, 69, 104, 117, 149, 153
West 5, 9, 11, 14, 15, 29, 33, 35, 36, 49, 51, 52, 53, 55, 57, 60, 62, 63, 65, 66, 67, 68, 69, 70, 71, 73, 76, 77, 78, 79, 84, 88, 89, 97, 98, 99, 100, 101, 102, 103, 104, 105, 106, 107, 108, 113, 115, 116, 118, 119, 121, 122, 123, 136, 137, 139
   Western 5, 10, 11, 12, 14, 15, 19, 23, 30, 33, 34, 36, 38, 41, 45, 51, 53, 56, 59, 60, 61, 63, 64, 65, 66, 67, 68, 69, 70, 71, 72, 73, 74, 75, 76, 77, 78, 84, 96, 97, 101, 111, 117, 118, 134, 139
   Westerness 65, 69, 74, 78, 79
Wołowiec 70, 84, 88, 90, 96, 99, 101, 104, 105, 108, 123, 128, 129, 132, 147, 154
work 10, 27, 31, 34, 36, 37, 41, 44, 45, 46, 58, 61, 88, 90, 101, 104, 106, 117, 123, 142, 148, 149
world 14, 15, 19, 29, 33, 35, 42, 44, 45, 56, 59, 64, 91, 100, 102, 106, 107, 110, 115, 118, 119, 120, 121
Wrocław 55, 65, 72, 81, 82, 94, 95, 111, 124, 125, 129, 148

Literatur und Kultur im mittleren und östlichen Europa

herausgegeben von Reinhard Ibler

ISSN 2195-1497

1 *Elisa-Maria Hiemer*
  Generationenkonflikt und Gedächtnistradierung
  Die Aufarbeitung des Holocaust in der polnischen Erzählprosa des 21. Jahrhunderts
  ISBN 978-3-8382-0394-2

2 *Adam Jarosz*
  Przybyszewski und Japan
  Bezüge und Annäherungen
  Mit einem Vorwort von Hanna Ratuszna und Quellentexten in Erstübertragung
  ISBN 978-3-8382-0436-9

3 *Adam Jarosz*
  Das Todesmotiv im Drama von Stanisław Przybyszewski
  ISBN 978-3-8382-0496-3

4 *Valentina Kaptayn*
  Zwischen Tabu und Trauma
  Kateřina Tučkovás Roman *Vyhnání Gerty Schnirch* im Kontext der tschechischen Literatur über die Vertreibung der Deutschen
  ISBN 978-3-8382-0482-6

5 *Reinhard Ibler (Hg.)*
  Der Holocaust in den mitteleuropäischen
  Literaturen und Kulturen seit 1989
  The Holocaust in the Central European Literatures and Cultures since 1989
  ISBN 978-3-8382-0512-0

6 *Iris Bauer*
  Schreiben über den Holocaust
  Zur literarischen Kommunikation in Marian Pankowskis Erzählung *Nie ma Żydówki*
  ISBN 978-3-8382-0587-8

7   *Olga Zitová*
    Thomas Mann und Ivan Olbracht
    Der Einfluss von Manns Mythoskonzeption auf die karpatoukrainische Prosa des tschechischen Schriftstellers
    ISBN 978-3-8382-0633-2

8   *Trixi Jansen*
    Der Tod und das Mädchen
    Eine Analyse des Paradigmas aus Tod und Weiblichkeit in ausgewählten Erzählungen I.S. Turgenev
    ISBN 978-3-8382-0627-1

9   *Olena Sivuda*
    "Aber plötzlich war mir, als drohe das Haus über mir zusammenzubrechen."
    Komparative Analyse des Heimkehrermotivs in der deutschen und russischen Prosa nach dem Zweiten Weltkrieg
    ISBN 978-3-8382-0779-7

10 *Victoria Oldenburger*
    Keine Menschen, sondern ganz besondere Wesen ...
    Die Frau als Objekt unkonventioneller Faszination in Ivan A. Bunins Erzählband
    Temnye allei (1937–1949)
    ISBN 978-3-8382-0777-3

11 *Andrea Meyer-Fraatz, Thomas Schmidt (Hg.)*
    „Ich kann es nicht fassen,
    dass dies Menschen möglich ist"
    Zur Rolle des Emotionalen in der polnischen Literatur über den Holocaust
    ISBN 978-3-8382-0859-6

12 *Julia Friedmann*
    Von der Gorbimanie zur Putinphobie?
    Ursachen und Folgen medialer Politisierung
    ISBN 978-3-8382-0936-4

13 Reinhard Ibler (Hg.)
    Der Holocaust in den mitteleuropäischen Literaturen und Kulturen:
    Probleme der Politisierung und Ästhetisierung
    The Holocaust in the Central European Literatures and Cultures:
    Problems of Poetization and Aestheticization
    ISBN 978-3-8382-0952-4

14 Alexander Lell
    Studien zum erzählerischen Schaffen Vsevolod M. Garšins
    Zur Betrachtung des Unrechts in seinen Werken aus der Willensperspektive
    Arthur Schopenhauers
    ISBN 978-3-8382-1042-1

15 Dmitry Shlapentokh
    The Mongol Conquests in the Novels of Vasily Yan
    An Intellectual Biography
    ISBN 978-3-8382-1017-9

16 Katharina Bauer
    Liebe – Glaube – Russland:
    Russlandkonzeptionen im Schaffen Aleksej N. Tolstojs
    ISBN 978-3-8382-1182-4

17 Magdalena Baran-Szołtys, Monika Glosowitz,
    Aleksandra Konarzewska (eds.)
    Imagined Geographies
    Central European Spatial Narratives between 1984 and 2014
    ISBN 978-3-8382-1225-8

18 Adam Jarosz
    Der Spiegel und die Spiegelungen
    Über Geschlecht und Seele im Werk von Stanisław Przybyszewski
    ISBN 978-3-8382-1246-3

ibidem.eu